DATE DUE			
JAN 1978			
Dec 19			
FEB			
Dec 17 78			
T.S.C			
MAR 1980			
DUE MAR 19 1981			
DUE APR 14 1981			
DEC 1985			
NOV 30 1987			
APR 28			
JUN 5 1997			

Rock Is Rhythm and Blues

(The Impact of Mass Media)

ROCK

IS RHYTHM

AND BLUES

(The Impact of Mass Media)

by

LAWRENCE N. REDD

MICHIGAN STATE UNIVERSITY PRESS

1974

★ ★
 ★
★ ★
 ★

ML
3556
R35

IN MEMORY OF
Elsie Mae Redd

Contents

Foreword

RECENTLY WE HAVE WITNESSED THE BEGINNING OF A NEW INterpretation of American history that is the direct outgrowth of the civil rights movement of the sixties and early seventies. Responding to pressures applied by the movement, historians have begun to write the true history of America. As a result, the contributions of blacks to America's cultural development are at long last becoming apparent. The historical sins of commission, which were also of omission, are finally beginning to be corrected.

Prior to the civil rights movement much of the historical material had been written by authors who: (1) lacked knowledge of the contributions of blacks; (2) knew of the contributions of blacks but failed to include these in their writings; or (3) were insensitive to or culturally different from blacks. The latter is the case of many authors who wrote about American popular music. As Leroi Jones pointed out in *Black Music,* "Black music has always been evaluated negatively; for, although its artists are black, its critics are invariably white."

Prior to this present work, popular music has always been divided into three separate idioms: jazz, rock and roll, and rhythm and blues. Both rock and roll and rhythm and blues have claimed some relationship to jazz, but not to each other. Authors, as well as film, radio, and television producers—who are mostly white—have denied or been unaware of the relationship between rock and rhythm and blues. They have failed to recognize, as Lawrence Redd points out, that: "Every black person immersed in his culture, knows that rock music is the creation of black people. The only real difference between what is called rock and roll, or pop music, and rhythm and blues, or soul music, was the failure of white performers to do the music justice in their initial performances."

Rock Music Is Rhythm and Blues is the product of intensive scholarly research and a lifetime of involvement with popular music. It investigates the roots of rhythm and blues (rock and roll) and the causes surrounding the dichotomy between the two terms. Even the phrase "rock and roll" has a black origin in rhythm and blues lyrics.

In tracing rhythm and blues back to African work songs, blues, and jazz, the author discusses the contributions of many early rhythm and blues pioneers. He recognizes radio's impact on the popularity of rhythm and blues and the acceptance of the term "rock and roll" via the white disc jockey Alan Freed. He also relates the importance of black disc jockeys and "black radio" and their special role in popularizing rhythm and blues.

In exploring the influence of the motion picture industry on rhythm and blues, the author gives special attention to the movies of Louis Jordan and the song "Rock Around the Clock," along with the resulting musical revolution. He reveals facts about early television programing practices for blacks and rhythm and blues. He concludes the television chapter with the TV appearance of Elvis Presley in the spring of 1956, establishing Presley (along with most white rock and roll singers) as a white carbon copy of Bo Diddley and other black rhythm and blues artists.

The second part of the book consists of interviews with six famous rhythm and blues pioneers: B. B. King, Brownie McGhee, Dave Clark, Arthur "Big Boy" Crudup, Jerry Butler, and Jessie Whitaker. Each of these artists substantiates and validates the conclusions drawn by Redd in *Rock Music Is Rhythm and Blues.*

Here, then, is a fresh, true look at popular music. It is written for students, teachers, disc jockeys, television and film producers, or anyone who listens to popular music. Readable and understandable, it reports the facts, straightforwardly, with "no-holds-barred." *Rock Music Is Rhythm and Blues* is a new book written about an old truth.

March 1974   WARRICK CARTER
                                           Governor's State University
                                           EDDIE MEADOWS
                                           San Diego State College

Preface

"BLUES IS BLUES," SAYS B. B. KING, AND TO THAT WE SHOULD properly add, "rock and roll is rhythm and blues." America has long separated rhythm and blues, a single musical idiom, into rock and roll as a euphemism for white, with rhythm and blues indicating black. And for far too long America has, for the most part, credited young white America with creating rock and roll, thereby robbing black America and many of its talented creators of a treasured part of their cultural heritage.

Historically, the rural, uneducated, and suppressed African-Americans in the South gave birth to the blues, and created rhythm and blues or, if you prefer, rock and roll. Africans and their descendants composed and sang work-songs from the motherland as they slaved to help build this nation. And the elements of their music— a strong beat, improvised rhythm, and call and response—had their roots in Africa. Early blues, or country blues as they later became known, were songs of lament for the suffering, oppression, and pain that the blacks shared with each other. Whether black men and women expressed their experiences in the field or in the Christian church, the music was African.

As black people moved from the rural areas into the cities, the country blues assumed an urban flavor. The music wedded with jazz and became universal in its expression, encompassing joy as well as depression.

Emerging in the 1920s, the blues remained separated from the mainstream of American culture by this nation's segregation patterns. Recordings of African-Americans were advertised as "race records" and sold well enough to establish a strong economic territory. Eventually, films with renowned black artists were released, but seldom to white-oriented theaters. Post World War II black pride led to protests over the stigma of "race records," and *Billboard* began calling the music "rhythm and blues." And by 1948 at least one radio station in America began to broadcast the music on a full-time scale.

In the fifties, with the first great upsurge of rhythm and blues into the white market, an increasing number of white-oriented radio stations aired rhythm and blues records. Then came the flood of imitators. Catchy rhythm and blues songs recorded by black artists

were copied by white-oriented recording companies using white artists. Many white-oriented stations chose to play the white versions
of rhythm and blues songs, which then climbed to the top of the
charts ahead of the original rhythm and blues recordings. Despite the
copying, African-American rhythm and blues recordings continued
to gain in popularity.

"Rock and roll," an African-American term used in rhythm and
blues lyrics, came to be used interchangeably with rhythm and blues.
Outside of show business, few people ever read. magazines of the
trade; if they did, they would have clearly observed the synonymous
use of rhythm and blues and rock and roll. Nonetheless, Alan Freed
in *Look* on June 26, 1956, revealed to millions of Americans that to
him rock and roll and rhythm and blues were synonymous.

> The old-timers who formerly controlled the music publishing business
> wouldn't even license rhythm and blues material until about a year ago. By
> that time a new group of writers and publishers had the inside track on rock
> and roll, and now the newcomers are making the money.

It was radio that catapulted rhythm and blues into national prominence and bigtime money. And it was the motion picture industry,
with films such as *Blackboard Jungle* and *Rock Around the Clock,*
which rocketed rhythm and blues on to the international scene. By
February 1956 *Billboard* was announcing: ". . . this is rhythm and
blues' greatest era. The idiom has come along with such overwhelming force as to leave no doubts of its validity as a major contribution
to the American scene."

Almost at the moment that African-Americans were about to
receive recognition for this musical contribution to the American
culture, the term rock and roll took on a new association, Elvis
Presley. In the spring of 1956, Presley, steeped in the music and
choreography of black rhythm and blues artists, wiggled and mumbled his way across the television screen. Young white America had
a new idol, and rock and roll began to assume an identity apart from
rhythm and blues. Radio, films, and television all got on the rock and
roll bandwagon, with too many program and music directors viewing rock and roll and rhythm and blues as separate creations. Not
knowing the real history, young white America was claiming rock
and roll as its own musical culture by the end of 1956.

Mass media, including the press, had created a false dichotomy.

Not until the Beatles, the Animals, the Rolling Stones, and other popular English singing groups gave full recognition and credit to black rhythm and blues artists for teaching them their musical styles did the dawn of truth begin to break.

The media that use rock and roll music cater to a young audience which has proclaimed love, peace, and the brotherhood of man as its philosophy of life. The young people demand that their music and its creators be real and honest. Accordingly, the role of the broadcasters and film producers should be one that reflects a consummated programing philosophy permeated with integrity and respect for all mankind.

It is time that every white person learn what every black person immersed in his culture knows—that rock music is really the creation of black people. The only real difference between what is now called rock and roll, or pop music, and rhythm and blues, or soul music, was the failure of white performers to do justice to the rhythm and blues music in their initial performances. Elvis Presley was an eclectic white carbon copy of black Bo Diddley and other famous rhythm and blues artists. Bill Haley's "Rock Around the Clock" was a copy of Sonny Dae's original. Even the term "rock and roll" was a part of the African-American language, a part of rhythm and blues lyrics, and that is where Alan Freed obtained the name for his radio show.

Because white America, through its mass communications media, has failed to give proper credit to the source of its pop music, it is guilty of robbing black America of one of its most treasured possessions—rhythm and blues.

The black experience of living and growing up in America provides the most important empirical data essential to the position that rhythm and blues and rock and roll are one and the same thing. Rocking church choirs and those old gospel recordings of the Pilgrim Travelers, the Clara Ward Singers, the Dixie Hummingbirds, and the Soul Stirrers are more than just memories. They are fortified cultural nuggets of soulful black Sunday mornings. Together with the music of secular groups—such as the Cadillacs, the Five Royals, the Dominoes, the Orioles—and of singles artists—such as Ruth Brown, Faye Adams, and the late Chuck Willis—life was made easier and more enjoyable for the souls of black folks. The experiences associated with those memories are constant reminders that rock and roll exists because rhythm and blues is its life and blood.

My own personal interest in the terms "rhythm and blues" and "rock" began in 1960 when I moved to Nashville to study at Tennessee State University. WVOL, the black station there, played music that the announcers called "rhythm and blues." The two Top 40 white stations, WMAK and WKDA, referred to their music as "rock." Both terms were new to me. All I had ever known was the blues and rock and roll, which I considered the same. I had grown up in Michigan with the assumption that the music played by black and whites was not really different, but for some reason whites preferred to call the blues "rock and roll."

As a senior at Tennessee State, I went to work as an announcer with WVOL, which was staffed by a number of successful black broadcasters: Morgan Babb, Ed Hall, Chuck Mitchell, E. Manny Clark, Jay Butler, Wash Allen, Clarence Kilcrest, Noble Blackwell, Al Johnson, and the late Joe Norfleet. Kilcrest and Johnson taught me enough about radio to get me a weekend news slot on Saturdays, and in the spring of 1964 Wash Allen recommended me for his disc jockey position when he took a job in Cleveland, Ohio.

That promotion permitted me to take a limited but serious interest in the singing career of Freddie North and eventually to challenging the separation between rock and roll and rhythm and blues. I got acquainted with Freddie through the Tennessee State University Players Guild, where we both were studying under the famous black collegiate director, Dr. Thomas E. Poag.

About a month before I left the radio station, I invited Freddie North to WVOL for an interview and an unveiling of his latest recording of "The Hurt" and "It's No Good for Me." When I returned to my home town, Grand Rapids, I took several of Freddie's records along to drop off at the local Top 40 stations.

The disc jockey at WLAV, Larry Adderly, who later became a Detroit sportscaster, listened to Freddie's record and informed me that this was a rhythm and blues platter and that Grand Rapids was a rock and roll area. I thought he was really saying that because Freddie was black, or sounded black, he was not going to program the record. I left WLAV very confused, since I had heard Martha and the Vandellas over that station.

My next stop was WMAX, where Bob Robin was the disc jockey. He also explained to me that he was not going to play Freddie's record because it was rhythm and blues, not rock and roll.

Had my roots in African-American music been shallow, I might then have been convinced that these Top 40 disc jockeys were correct. However, I had taken more than Freddie's record with me to those radio stations. I had brought a black music experience which began when I was a child in an old four-room shack that sat in the middle of a dusty cotton patch, a few miles south of Blythville, Arkansas. Every afternoon I positioned myself in front of a battery-powered radio and waited for a deep voice to sing "Sorrow Valley." That was my initial baptism into the music of my African-American culture.

After World War II my parents moved to Michigan, where we lived with my Aunt Rosie. Soon after our arrival, my aunt bought a combination radio and phonograph. To celebrate the occasion, my mother purchased a recording, "Choo Choo Cha Boogie," by Louis Jordan. Later she bought me a recording of "Open the Door Richard," as well as just about every song Louis Jordan recorded.

Music was everywhere around me, and I listened to it all. At the stage door of the Horse Shoe Bar, behind my grandfather's house, I heard name bands such as Buddy Johnson, famous for the song "Since I Fell for You" and at that time music director of Atlantic Records. At my Aunt Helen's restaurant I listened to the juke box recordings of the great Amos Milburn and his "Bad bad whiskey made me lose my happy home," Ruth Brown and her "Every time it rains I think of you and tears drop from my eyes," and Peppermint Harris and his "I got loaded. Lord, I sure got high."

On rainy days or whenever I was lonesome, old 78 rpm records were the best friends I had. I would spend hours playing Johnny Moore and the Three Blazers, Lowell Fulson, Big Bill Broonzy and his Chicago Five, Jack McVey and his All Stars, Larry Darnell, Louis Jordan, and especially Ivory Joe Hunter's "S. P. Blues." I memorized each artist and his record label, noticing writers such as Percy Mayfield, Charles Brown, Jessie Mae Robinson, and Joe Liggins. From that record collection I learned about music and to appreciate the blues and gospel singing.

While at WVOL in Nashville, Morgan Babb and Ed Hall, two fine musicologists on that station's staff, helped to educate me in the history of blues, gospel, and rhythm and blues. Morgan was one of the original members of the Radio Four gospel recording group, and Ed was guitarist for a local Nashville gospel group. Through Morgan and Ed I came to understand the evolution of dance routines that began with gospel groups and then taken over by secular vocal recording artists. Through Morgan and Ed I learned about the remarkable blues bands that would spread throughout an audience without losing a beat, about the importance of the late Little Walter, and about the legends of Sonny Boy Williamson, "Big Boy" Crudup, the Fairfield Four, and, most important, the great T-Bone Walker.

I was so shocked by the Freddie North experience that it stimulated me to recall a very important incident that had happened on television a few years back. During the height of the Twist, Hank Ballard and two other African-Americans were guests on the television show "To Tell the Truth." The questions were distributed evenly among the guests until Hank was asked, "What is the difference between rhythm and blues and rock and roll?" He answered that rhythm and blues and rock and roll were all the same, that there was no difference. After that answer, Hank Ballard, who was as well-known to young blacks as Frank Sinatra was to everyone, was never asked another question by the all-white panel. He received no votes as the creator of the Twist, while an offensive end for the New York Giants football team received three votes as the originator of the song and dance. It was obvious that Ballard had been eliminated because of his remarks on rock and roll and rhythm and blues.

Armed with an oral history of music and the black experiences of my youth, I began to document my position that rhythm and blues and rock and roll are one and the same. Although the reason for the split eluded me, avenues in my own environment began to open up and encourage my research. A childhood friend, Harry T. Lewis, Jr., was managing the great blues man T-Bone Walker and he brought T-Bone to Grand Rapids for a performance. I arranged an interview with him. The Dixie Hummingbirds gospel quartet were gracious and encouraging during an interview on gospel quartet history. And finally Lewis booked B. B. King into Grand Rapids. During an interview before his performance in 1965, the king of blues, a one-time disc jockey at Memphis radio station WDIA, pointed me in the proper direction. Although the technology had surrounded me, I had not realized the power and impact of radio. Consequently, when I entered Michigan State University a few years later to do graduate study in television and radio, I pursued to research the relationship between rhythm and blues and broadcasting.

Grand Rapids, Michigan   LAWRENCE N. REDD

Acknowledgments

THE AUTHOR HEREBY WISHES TO ACKNOWLEDGE THOSE PERSONS who were very helpful to me when this book was still a fragile idea: Jerry and Willie Nelson, Patricia Pullium, Peggy Lawson, and William Cheaney for their positive feedback and time; LaNelle Roman, Drs. Eddie Meadows and Warrick Carter, and Andrena Gist for encouraging my research by inviting me to lecture in their black history and music classes; Bert and Louise Price, John and Beverly Matthews, John Butler, Herman Morrow, and Nathel Burtley for their valuable cooperation, support, and encouragement. Drs. William Green, Peter Flynn, Terrell Taylor, and Thomas Foster for the many long discussions on the generalizability of the work on a sociological level; and to all of those who were unable to escape my crusade, I offer my heartfelt gratitude.

Many persons shared their valuable collection of old 78 rpm records that I studied, and I am deeply indebted to: Hardie and Louise Farr, Emery Baskins, Al and Beatrice Roberts, Maggie Baskins, and the Reverend Herbert Taylor. To Alexander Payne, William Edmondson and his wife, Barbara, I am especially grateful for the broadcasting and recording sources they acquired for me.

For my baptism into the music, long before I recognized its importance, I wish to acknowledge my parents, Elsie and Andrew Redd; and for my musical environment: Helen and Hermon McElwee, Helen and Wesley Johnson, Rosie Lee Morris, Ola and Joe Henry, and Thermon McElwee.

The following broadcasters are appreciated for their responses to survey inquiries which provided valuable historical information on radio programming as well as encouragement to pursue the research effort: Robert B. Q. Burris of KATL in St. Louis; Tom Maxwell of WIBB in Macon, Georgia; E. Rodney Jones of WVON in Chicago; Jimmy Byrd of WILD in Boston; Guy Cameron of WUFO in Buffalo; E. Manny Clark of WGIV in Charlotte, North Carolina; Ervin Hester of WRSC in Durham, North Carolina; Dick Starr of WFUN in Miami; Robert (Honeyboy) Thomas of WDIA in Memphis; Randy Warren of WLOK in Memphis; Wayne Rink of WJAK in Jackson, Tennessee; Jim (Dandy) Rucker of WLOU in Louisville; Robert Morgan of WBOP in Pensacola; and William Brown of

WJET of Beaumont, Texas. In addition, I am grateful to Thomas Carroll of Shaw Artists for information on recording artists and for his encouragement.

I cannot say enough about the late Mr. Leo Martin. Mr. Martin's initial approval of my thesis proposal and his thoughtful criticisms in the early stages of the work cast an indelible broadcasting imprint upon this book that is deeply appreciated and respected. Equally, much gratitude is expressed to Dr. Robert Schlater, who succeeded Mr. Martin as department chairman at Michigan State University, and advisor to my work, for his continuing guidance, criticism, and assurance throughout the development of the book. And personal acknowledgement is given to Dr. Thomas Baldwin for his valuable resources, encouragement, information leads, and personal assistance with the work.

To the artists whose interviews are included in this book, I am deeply indebted. All were very gracious in giving me their valuable time as well as leads on research information. In addition, I express my appreciation to the Michigan State University Department for Urban Affairs for the permission to use the interviews of Jerry Butler and Dave Clark in this book. Early in my efforts, the Dixie Hummingbirds, Riley "B. B." King, and Arron "T-Bone" Walker granted me interviews and helped me to comprehend the scope of my endeavor. Although their interviews were not recorded, their inspiration to this book cannot be measured.

I am appreciative to the poet and historian, Richard Thomas, for his constant insistance that I continue to seek a publisher. The editorial comments of Gerald Elliott and David Nicolette of the *Grand Rapids Press* were invaluable and Wilma Moody was of great assistance during the early stages of my effort. In the final analysis, Jean Busfield and Lyle Blair of the Michigan State University Press have been tremendous in their efforts to bring this book to life.

There are numerous other persons who have assisted me in this endeavor who for lack of space and time are not mentioned. I must, however, offer a very special thanks to my wife, Betty, for her patience, understanding and support, and to Mr. Johnny Johnson, a truly outstanding musicologist.

PART ONE

Blues Is Blues

CHAPTER 1.

Birth of the Blues

Where the Blues Began

THE BLUES WERE BORN ON RAILROAD GANGS, IN LUMBER CAMPS, in cotton fields, on ocean docks and river boats, and in black settlings of southern plantations and were created by the rural, uneducated, and most suppressed and unprepared black freedom seekers. There they were discovered in the early 1900s by people who could advance the music to the forefront. The musical elements—a strong beat, improvised rhythm, and call and response—were not created in America but were adapted to the instruments found here and shaped into a new form by African slaves and their descendants, through the blood, sweat, and tears they had to shed to survive in America.

Trudging behind a plow under the boiling sun, Africans composed native music as they stumbled over clods of earth, toiling six and often seven days a week before the sun came up until after it went down. Slaves who picked cotton composed rhythmic songs with a beat which helped to ease the pain by distracting their minds from their backbreaking work. Across the fields they called to each other, in hollers and often in cries of pain. These soul sounds moaned across the Southland seeking someone to relate their troubles. Africans needed a safety valve to release the pain, and their music became their savoir.

Many times the cotton bundles were so heavy that it required a team of slaves to do one chore. As they toiled, black men composed jungle work-songs of their homeland, with an emphasized beat placed at certain notes in a rhythm. At the same time the stressed notes were sung, everyone pulled, pushed, or lifted to get the work done. The song always had a story, and a lead singer would work a rhythm around and between the motions of the workers until each ebony slave was in completely synchronized movements, singing and toiling. They used riffs, short musical phrases which were repeated over and over and tossed back and forth between the leader and the work crew.

Work Song

LEADER: Oh, baby Ugh! what you gonna do? Ugh!
        Three C Railroad Ugh! done run through! Ugh!
WORK-   Me and my pardner, Ugh! him and me! Ugh!
  GANG: Him and M-e-e Ugh! him and me! Ugh!
        Him and me! Ugh!

LEADER: Oh, baby, Ugh! what you gonna do? Ugh!
        Seaboard Air-line Ugh! done run through! Ugh!

WORK-   Me and my pardner, Ugh! him and me! Ugh!
  GANG: Him and me-e-e Ugh! him and me! Ugh!
        Him and me! Ugh!

LEADER: Oh baby, Ugh! what you gonna do? Ugh!
        B and O Railroad Ugh! done run through! Ugh![1]

After the Civil War Africans who stayed on plantations continued to suffer, as did those who left. Many wound up on prison work farms, an extension of slavery to preserve the cheap labor force. Wherever they were, the black men usually slaved seven days a week. It was rough toiling on river boats, chain gangs, and ocean docks. It was slave labor "calling track" on railroad gangs under the scorching sun. But as the black men drudged, they continued to compose songs and to sing. All day long a work leader sang a statement, the work gang repeated it; the work leader sang a statement, the work gang added to it; the work leader sang a statement, the work gang exclaimed about it. They slid into their notes; their voices swooped around and under notes, playing with them, refusing to hit them straight on. They paused to create more lyrics, while the rhythm and beat continued to work.

Then, finally it happened. Under those painful conditions the blues began to surface. LeRoi Jones in his famous work entitled *Blues People* succinctly describes a logical evolution of the music:

Very early blues did not have the "classic" twelve-bar, three-line, AAB
structure. For a while . . . blues-type songs utilized the structure of the early
English ballad, and sometimes these songs were eight, ten, or sixteen bars.
The shout as much as the African call-and-response singing dictated the form
blues took. Blues issued directly out of the shout and, of course, the spiritual.
The three-line structure of the blues was a feature of the shout. The first two
lines of the song were repeated, it would seem, while the singer was waiting
for the next line to come. Or, as was characteristic of the hollers and shouts,
the single line could be repeated again and again, either because the singer
especially liked it, or because he could not think of another line. The repeated
phrase also carries into instrumental jazz as the riff.[2]

The ring shout was a shuffling ceremonial dance African slaves
brought from their native land. They shuffled around in a counter-
clockwise circle as participants chanted and clapped hands. The
accent and emphasis was upon rhythm more than on melody. Some
persons sang as they danced, while others clapped their hands and
stomped their feet. (The spirit of the ring shout is well preserved in
black Christian churches today.) The repetitious musical phrases
and body movements created a hypnotic effect upon the participants.
As the dance progressed in speed and intensity, flavored with improvised syncopation, the dancers became possessed with the Spirit,
screamed and shouted, and flung themselves joyously in complete
spiritual ecstasy.

However, the gay, happy-go-lucky, sleepy-eyed slave, singing,
dancing, and joking in nineteenth century minstrel shows, signified
the only side of those ebony human beings that the white people at
that time in this nation's history wanted to see. The serious side of
the African-Americans was for decades plus scores intentionally
overlooked and thought unimportant, to say the least.

Popularity of the Blues

It took the "Father of the Blues," W. C. Handy, a black minstrel,
and Ma Rainey, who discovered and groomed the great Bessie Smith,
to emphasize to the world that black secular music had humanness.
However, Mr. Handy and the first of the great female blues singers,
Mrs. Rainey, first had to be convinced themselves. Handy, an educated man, read and wrote music, was city raised, and was a leader
of a big band which traveled with Mahara's Minstrels, an all-black

show. Just as white men discovered gold among the slaves when they founded the minstrel show, so in 1903 Handy, a one-time college professor, discovered gold among his black country brothers of Mississippi. He abandoned imitating black imitators, and like a thirsty man at sea cast down his bucket for the real thing:

> I hasten to confess that I took up with low folk forms hesitantly. . . . As a director of many respectable, conventional bands, it was not easy for me to concede that a simple slow drag and repeat could be rhythm itself. . . . My own enlightenment came in Cleveland, Mississippi. I was leading the orchestra in a dance program when someone sent up an odd request. Would we play some of "our native music," the note asked. This baffled me. . . . A few moments later a second request came up. Would we object if a local colored band played a few dances? Object! That was funny. What hornblower would object to a time out and smoke on pay? We eased out gracefully as the new-comers entered. They were led by a long-legged chocolate boy, and their band consisted of just three pieces, a battered guitar, and mandolin, and a worn-out bass.
>
> The music they made was pretty well in keeping with their looks. They struck up one of those over-and-over strains that seem to have no very clear beginning and certainly no ending at all. The strumming attained a disturbing monotony, but on and on it went. . . . A rain of silver dollars began to fall around the outlandish, stomping feet. The dancers went wild. Dollars, quarters, halves . . . the shower grew and continued so long I strained my neck to get a better look. There before the boys lay more money than my nine musicians were being paid for the entire engagement. Then I saw the beauty of primitive music.[3]

Unlike the black grassroots people who created and enjoyed the music initially, Handy was educated and wrote the music down. In Dorothy Scarborough's *On the Trail of Negro Folk Songs,* Handy gives credit for the blues to his culture:

> Each one of my blues is based on some old Negro song of the South, some folk song that I heard from my mammy when I was a child. Something that sticks in my mind that I hum to myself when I'm not thinking about it. Some old song that is part of the memories of my childhood and my race. I can tell you the exact song I used as the basis for any one of my blues.[4]

While traveling with a tent show in the Southwest one year earlier Ma Rainey heard the blues as recounted by John Work in 1940.

> Ma Rainey heard them in 1902 in a small town in Missouri where she was appearing with a show under a tent. She tells of a girl from the town who came to the tent one morning and began to sing about "the man" who left her. The

song was so strangely poignant that it attracted much attention. Ma Rainey became so interested that she learned the song from the visitor, and used it soon afterwards in her "act" as an encore.

The song elicited such response from the audiences that it won a special place in her act. Many times she was asked what kind of song it was, and one day she replied, in a moment of inspiration, "it's the blues."

She added, however, that after she began to sing the blues, although they were not so named then, she frequently heard similar songs in the course of her travels.[5]

The blues began to emerge in the early 1900s from a multitude of rural black male folk singers. Often the songs were sung by prisoners and by guitar players, who drifted from place to place seeking work, and frequently finding it by entertaining other black men in labor camps. The blues became a music between a black man with plenty of trouble and his understanding guitar and the lyrics attain their wealth in the soul of the layman digging and chipping away at an insolvable problem of life: somewhere to go but no way to get there, a pressing debt but no money to pay it, a desire to love but only a cold and empty world to embrace, or a thirst to relax but no place to rest.

I've Been Treated Wrong

I don't know my real name, I don't know where I was born.
  (repeat)
The troubles I been having seems like I was raised in an orphan
  home.

My mother died and left me when I was only two years old,
  (repeat)
And the troubles I been having the good Lord only knows.

I been treated like an orphan and worked just like a slave,
  (repeat)
If I never get my revenge evilness will carry me to my grave.

Now I been having trouble ever since I been grown.
  (repeat)
I'm too old for the orphan and too young for the old folks' home.[6]

Perry Bradford, as a young black growing up in the South at the turn of the century, heard black prisoners singing these soulful songs. His home was located next door to the Atlanta jail, and he was intrigued by the prisoners' music. Later, as a young musician in New York, who had traveled the country, Bradford desperately tried to convince record companies to record some of the blues songs. He related his efforts in his colorful book *Born With The Blues:*

> I tramped the pavements of Broadway with the belief that the country was waiting for the sound of the voice of a Negro singing the blues with a Negro Jazz combination playing for her. I felt strongly it should be a girl and that was what I was trying to sell. I was laughed at by all the wise guys in Tin Pan Alley. I had pleaded with Columbia and Victor companies to issue a record of a Negro girl. Though they were attentive, there was "no dice" after the "conference" with Executives.
>
> . . . but I was too stubborn to give up the idea because I had traveled all over the country singing and playing the blues. And I knew the people were waiting for that sound on the record because it was the sound of America, Negro and White.
>
> The South was especially crazy about the blues, a cry of a broken heart that echoed from every levee and bayou up and down the Mississippi River. It was a "cry," but still the outburst seemed to ease the pain.[7]

Finally, Bradford convinced the Okeh Record Company to record Mamie Smith, a beautiful black woman from Cincinnati, singing a blues number he had written. So on August 10, 1920,

> . . . she cut Bradford's "Crazy Blues" with its choruses based on a twelve-bar structure, the first vocal recording to employ a blues form. For months the disc sold some 7,500 copies a week, revealing the existence of a market that the record companies were not slow to exploit. In Alberta Hunter's words, Mamie Smith "made it possible for all of us."[8]

This explains why, rather than recording the real male country blues, the record companies at first recorded black females singing a smoother style that was to become known as classic blues. Mamie Smith was soon to be forgotten, and names such as Ida Cox, Ma Rainey, and Bessie Smith were to reign. Not much is written about Ida Cox, but this author's father insists that she was one of the big three. Bessie Smith became the most popular female blues singer, although it was Rainey who discovered her in Chattanooga, Tennessee, and groomed her for show business. Bessie became known as "Empress of the Blues." Bessie's voice was similar to that of Mahalia

Jackson's, and the statuesque beauty of a handsome woman's painful cry could make empathy very easy with a frank song such as "Empty Bed Blues." Southern Jim Crow turned a serious automobile wreck into a fatal accident when Bessie could not get admittance to a white hospital because she was black.

Ma Rainey is monumental, for she was the first great female blues singer. One of her biggest hit songs, which she also wrote, was "See See Rider." She was married at sixteen to Will Rainey, who directed the famous Rabbit Foot Minstrels. She began her recording career in her mid-thirties and retired during the Depression. Before she died on December 22, 1939, she had established the vogue for female blues singers.

Record companies soon found that the blues by female vocalists were not the most sought-after music. Most blacks preferred the male country blues singer. In the meantime, Mamie Smith's recordings had made Okeh a major company. To meet the new demand for country blues, and yet keep "colored" music separated from white, Okeh coined the term "race records." Sam Charters maintains that Okeh recording director, Ralph Peer, created the stigma, which was to last well into the late forties: "Ralph Peer was trying to think of a catalog title for his new records, and rather than calling them 'Negro' records, decided on 'Race' records, and the name lasted."[9]

Record companies began selling millions of records to the "Race," Negroes. The 1920s were deluged by recorded blues: Falling Rain Blues; Looking Girl Blues; Too Light Blues; Down-Hearted Blues, the list is endless. Emerging in the early 1920s, from a forest of blues and work-song folk singers to nurture the country blues into popularity, were rough, country-styled singers such as PaPa Charlie Jackson, Gus Cannon, Hosie Woods, Furry Lewis, Will Shade, and a host of forgotten drifters who perfected clever interplay between themselves and their guitars.

The blues were everywhere there was a "ghetto," and the leading exponent became Blind Lemon Jefferson. Lemon was born sightless on a small farm just outside Wortham, Texas, in 1897. He had a gift for guitar picking, which was just about the only thing a blind, uneducated boy could do to earn a living. Neighbors taught him all they could, but most of the guitar learning Lemon got on his own, by singing and playing at picnics and parties. He went to Chicago by way of Dallas and began recording for Paramount Records in 1925. Though his records were most popular among blacks, he was never well paid. His sliding and swooping voice moaned and cried. Once his records became available, attempts to imitate his talking guitar were numerous. His impact on guitar players is still prevalent today.

One night after a recording session in the winter of 1930, Lemon left the studio and walked into a snowstorm. The next morning Blind Lemon Jefferson, with his guitar near his side, was found frozen to death. He had left a warm legacy of over seventy recordings behind, and a guarantee that the blues would never die—only change with the times.

Black people who had moved from the farm during and shortly after World War I began to adopt an urban style of living, and in the late twenties the country blues began to lose a bit of their vast popularity. The basic blues, however, were still very popular, although the sound began to soften and move toward what is basically referred to today as the urban blues vein.

Development of Rhythm and Blues

In 1928, at the encouragement of friends, a young singer-piano player left his native Nashville, Tennessee, home for the big city and bright lights of Chicago, to make a name for himself. The young man never wrote back to say how he was making out, but he did send word. It was a hit recording of "How Long, How Long Blues" which he was to rerecord six times before his death. The young man's name was Leroy Carr. And if you have ever heard the song of "In the Evening (when the sun goes down)," you have some idea of the great talent he possessed.

In Chicago Leroy met Francis "Scrapper" Blackwell. Together with Carr's smooth approach to playing piano and singing the blues and Blackwell's relaxed guitar playing, they completely influenced a new style of singing and playing the blues. According to Charles Keil, Leroy Carr's

. . . thoroughly citified and sophisticated blues style was immensely popular; in many ways the Carr-Blackwell recordings foreshadow the Kansas City florescence. Along with guitarist Lonnie Johnson, a thorough musician and technician from St. Louis, Scrapper Blackwell's single-string lines helped clear the way for the first electric guitarists, Eddie Durham and Charlie Christian of the Kansas City era. Carr's songs were used by Basie and Rushing in the late thirties; on some early recordings, Basie and his rhythm section do two of Carr's blues that show the influence of Carr's piano style as well. Many of today's bluesmen—B. B. King and Jimmy Witherspoon, for example, credit Carr and Blackwell as being two of the first modernists in the field.[10]

The urban blues matured and climaxed as a result of a combination which brought together country bluesmen who moved westward and swing era jazz bands of the Southwest. In the 1930s these itinerant Territory bands in the Southwest and Texas, where there was relatively greater musical freedom of expression, began to appear and finally culminated in Kansas City with a male blues vocalist as a permanent part of the jazz band.

Keil goes on to say of the Kansas City scene:

Many singers from the Kansas City phase were not instrumentalists, but relied upon a reed or brass player for responses to their vocal calls. Saxophonists in the Jay McShann band, which once included Charlie Parker, provided the foil to the singing of Walter Brown, Al Hibbler, and Jimmy Witherspoon; many of the instrumentalists in other bands came to be almost as well known as the vocalists they were paired with—trombonist Dickie Wells with Jimmy Rushing, pianist Pete Johnson with Joe Turner. . . . The modern blues style that these men epitomize was transformed and remolded after the war.[11]

The characteristics of the Kansas City style of male blues singers performing with heavy rhythmic jazz bands is described and compared with the earlier styles of Rainey, Smith, Cox, and Leroy Carr, by Raymond Horricks in *Count Basie and his Orchestra:*

The singing became suddenly more superficially energetic, more prone to aggression in its delivery, and so in keeping with the rhythmic excitement and attacking swing evidenced by the town's jazz groups. The blues song became more catholic in outlook, embracing all moods and all spirits, therefore suitable for the expression of excitement as well as depression. The dramatic, heart-searching dirge of Bessie Smith was replaced by the volatile driving song of Jimmy Rushing. Lyrics retained their message of outcry against a lost lover or against some oppressive action by the authorities, yet the phrases which propagated the stories took on a rhythmic force, edging closer than ever to the moulded, decorative phrases of a jazz instrumental solo. Make no mistake, the blues songs didn't lose their sincerity or their intensity. If anything, pushing the approach closer to the alive, swinging style of the Kansas City jazz unit served as a precautionary measure against undue elements of sophistication creeping in. Jimmy Rushing singing a blues at medium tempo above the emphatic beat of the Count Basie rhythm section didn't represent a dilution of the lament-type blues brought to perfection by performers such as Bessie Smith, Ma Rainey, Ida Cox, and Leroy Carr. If one considers the linking of the plaintive lyric with the force and delivery methods of a jazz group a crime, then Rushing could be adjudged guilty. Yet while he and others took on the spirit of jazz musicians, of the men with whom they worked, they still retained all the old intensity and feeling in their singing. If Rushing felt sad he sang a slow blues; but if he felt gay he didn't just stop singing, for fear of desecrating the blues form. Like the musician he used the blues for every mood and he worked constantly with jazz groups.[12]

Midway during World War II a young man from the Southwest, a Texan named Arron "T-Bone" Walker, began to rule a substantial share of blues popularity. He learned to play the blues from his father and uncle. As a young boy, he played guitar for a medicine show when school was not in session. This author interviewed T-Bone in March 1965 in Grand Rapids, Michigan. The pioneering blues singer pleasantly recalled the "Big B Tonic" by Doc Breeden. Although Breeden claimed the tonic would cure anything, T-Bone says it was only Black Draught. However, fifteen dollars a week was good money for a young boy, even though ten of it did go home.

T-Bone remembered leading Blind Lemon around several times, and from him he picked up some guitar pointers. He recorded at the age of sixteen, but his records were not very successful. Later in his career he played for Cab Calloway's big band. That was his shortest engagement. On his second night with the band, when he showed up late for work, he was fired.

T-Bone's smooth guitar style accompanied the great Ida Cox and also Ma Rainey on some of their recordings. Eventually his travels led him to California, where in 1939 he joined the Les Hite's orchestra. This was his biggest break.

That same year he went with the orchestra to New York and recorded "Wichita Blues." He formed his own band that had a heavy rhythmic flavor of the Southwest, which was reflected in the Kansas City movement. The recording led him to stardom, which was to last well over a decade. According to Morgan Babb, former program director of radio station WVOL in Nashville, Tennessee, T-Bone, as part of his dance routine while playing the guitar, would jump straight up in the air with his string instrument high above his head and come down in a split with his guitar behind his head but never losing a beat. Meanwhile, women in the audience would jump up, scream, and shout just like it was revival time. During the interview the author asked the famed bluesman if he still did the split. T-Bone smiled warmly, as if remembering the good times and said, "I do sometimes, but I am not as young as I used to be, you know." Charters maintains that Walker's dance routines were copied by many, including Bo Diddley, who was copied by Elvis Presley.[13]

T-Bone mastered the electric guitar at its early inception; and although Charlie Christian is considered the modern influencing electric guitarist, T-Bone was the first blues singer to achieve astounding success with it. He influenced many of the current blues singers employing the electric box. Of this influence Keil has also agreed:

> Although Wynonie Harris, Joe Turner, the Browns (Walter and Roy), and Percy Mayfield exerted considerable influence in the late forties and early fifties, T-Bone Walker and Louis Jordan seem to have had the greatest impact on their follow bluesmen.[14]

Louis Jordan will be discussed later.

T-Bone made several television appearances during the early 1950s and wrote one of Bobby Bland's biggest hits, "Stormy Monday Blues." If you ever hear the old heads mumbling "the eagle flies on Friday," it is because they remember the great Arron "T-Bone" Walker singing it in the mid-to-late 1940s.

Postwar years were boom years, and black people were risking their lives endeavoring to slip away from southern farms and plantations at night to journey North and West for a better life. Their work was at the bottom of the ladder, but living conditions were better, so they thought, and the money was good. Many were getting their "kicks on Route 66," as the King Cole Trio hit song suggested. Life was less restricting for the rural cultured blacks who moved to the city. The new freedom spirit attained by the heroic performance of blacks in the war and the new hope the world had in general was reflected in the music. It was truly a new day. The traditional country blues was out of style, and the new blues was more rhythmic. Jazz and blues had joined together. The Kansas City style was the new foundation on which to build free and swinging vocal blues.

Private Cecil Gant was singing "I Wonder." Joe Liggins wrote "The Honey Dripper," another big hit in 1945. And Helen Humes with Bill Doggett scored big with "Be-Ba-Ba-Luba." It was a period when Lionel Hampton was popular with "Hey! BA-BA-RE-Bop." The Mills Brothers continued their success with "Dream, Dream, Dream" and "Across the Alley From the Alamo." And Johnny Moore and His Three Blazers released "Merry Christmas Baby." Friends knocked on doors and yelled, "Caldonia! Caldonia! What makes your big head so hard," or hollered out, "Open the door, Richard!" The residents were not lost for words either. Often they replied, "Ain't nobody here but us chickens."

The greetings were from song titles, and Louis Jordan popularized two of the three. Jack McVea, the coauthor of "Open the Door Richard," had recorded that song. So many whites copied the song that people around the world knew about the man who could not get into his own house because Richard was asleep and had the only key.

Louis Jordan was a jazz saxophonist and leader of his own band, called the Tympany Five. Maud-Cuney Hare mentions him with the same tributes accorded Duke Ellington and Earl Hines in her 1936 book *Negro Musicians and Their Music.*[15] Jordan's home was Brinkley, Arkansas, which is about sixty miles from Memphis. Whatever happened in Kansas City first, soon happened in the Memphis area second. And when Kansas City began to slow down, Memphis became second in music only to Chicago. Jordan eventually moved to Chicago, but the Kansas City-Memphis influence was already working.

After the war and perhaps during that period Jordan's career began to bloom and spread in all directions, defying any classification of the day. Everything he was doing then is in vogue today. In April 1945 *Billboard* Magazine had this to say about Louis Jordan, then ascending to the peak of his career:

Theater "Talk"! The biggest Hit at the Paramount Theater, New York, in years! Completed first engagement Feb. 27, 1945—returned by demand June 13, 1945, and already booked for third return engagement nine months later.

Trade "Talk"! Jordan is a great showman—belongs at the top of the heap! This guy's good!—"Variety"—Jordan's all over the place singin', dancin', clownin', and totin' his sax. He packs in laughs and customers, to.. . . "Billboard".

Movie "Talk"! Louis Jordan is a natural showman. We are testing him for a comedy lead in one of our forthcoming pictures—Paramount Pictures.

Record "Talk"! Louis Jordan's recording with Bing Crosby of "My Baby Said Yes," and "Your Socks Don't Match" promises to be a real hit. Jordan's rendition of the novelty tune, "Caldonia" is great—Dave Kapp, Decca Records.

Song "Talk"! "Caldonia (what makes your big head so hard)" is the novelty hit of 1945 thanks to Louis Jordan's Decca recording and his terrific vocal rendition—Henry Spitzer, Morris Music.

Short "Talk"! Louis Jordan's an actor, too; his work in the musical short, "Caldonia," is superb—Wm. F. Crouch, Director.[16]

Jordan did not rest on his acclaim; he cut records with Ella Fitzgerald, Jimmy Dorsey, and Guy Lombardo. Wild Bill Davis arranged for him. He went on to record such hits as "Choo Choo Ch' Boogie," which sold a million, "Ain't That Just Like a Woman," which was recorded again by Elvis Presley in the sixties, "Don't Let the Sun Catch You Crying," and other famous hit songs such as "Beware," "Jack You're Dead," "Saturday Night Fish Fry," and "Beans and Cornbread."

People still talk about "letting the good times roll," primarily because Louis Jordan made a hit song out of it in 1946.

After World War II black people openly resented the label "race music," and in 1948 *Billboard* Magazine began calling the new blues rhythm and blues. Louis Jordan, even more so than Walker, was king of rhythm and blues. It swung, it had more jazz rhythms, it was intoxicated with greater freedom and had no clear direction as to where it was going—the music truly rocked. In 1948 Earskin Hawkins released "Blues After Hours," and black people adopted it as their national anthem. "Stick" McGhee was singing "Drinkin' Wine Spo-dee-o-dee," Roy Brown was "Rocking At Midnight," Jimmy Witherspoon made the charts with "No Rollin' Blues," Little Ester and Johnny Otis had twin hits, "Mistrustin' Blues" and "Double Crossing Blues," Lucky Millinder, who later became a disc jockey, arrived with "D' Natural Blues," and, Bull Moose Jackson softly crooned "All My Love Belongs to You."

Meanwhile, the African group work-song had retained its structure and emotional zeal in the black church in the form of gospel quartet singing, which was very popular, especially among southern blacks. Although gospel quartets, which preceded even the Fairfield Four, Golden Gate Quartet, and Delta Rhythm Boys, remain the least researched element of modern musical roots, their style and tradition gave birth to the secular quartet groups such as the famous Ink Spots, who also used the African work-song structure of a lead singer "call" and group "response." Their 1941 hit recording of "If I Didn't Care" sold over a million copies. By 1949 the secular work-song quartet style hit the rhythm and blues charts to stay.

Ebony magazine captured the late 1940s creation of the Orioles in a 1952 article which related how a white songwriter, Deborah Chester, telephoned a friend and discovered Sonny Til and his friends singing in the background:

> Excited, Deborah listened more closely, arranged to meet the Orioles (then called the Vibronaires). A week later, she had arranged an Arthur Godfrey audition in which they competed against a British pianist named George Shearing. The Orioles lost the Godfrey contest but twenty-four hours later, Deborah, back in her Baltimore home, received a frantic long-distance call from Godfrey.
>
> "The mail's piling up and the phones are going crazy," the famed talent scout shouted. "Everyone's saying the Orioles should have won and they won't drink any more Lipton's Tea. Bring them back to New York right away."
>
> The Godfrey triumph and waxing of a Deborah Chester tune *Too Soon to Know* sent the Orioles soaring to success.[17]

The African style of singing was so imitated, Chuck Lowery, ex-Pied Piper (the Pied Pipers held *Downbeat* poll honors for years and were part of the Tommy Dorsey Orchestra) stated in a 1953 *Downbeat* issue that most of the singing groups were lousy and that "those lousy Ink Spots started the decline. That Bill Kenny whining, with three nondescript so-called singers moaning in the background."[18]

Though Lowery may have been referring to current white groups, his mention of the Ink Spots as the genus of this African style of singing slightly off key to the European ear is important because it notes the African influence Kenny, Deek Watson, Charlie Fuqua, and Hoppy Jones had on the pop musical scene. More importantly, it was the secular quartet, because of their popularity, who brought attention to the rhythm and blues lyric phrase rock and roll, an African American expression popular among blacks for many years, which had deep roots in African-American music.

Rhythm and Blues Lyrics

Though it is not the purpose of this work to trace lyrics, it is necessary to establish the phrase rock and roll as an intrinsic part of the African-American language and rhythm and blues songs. The late Langston Hughes established a point of reference in his work, *The Big Sea,* when he told of a high society matron's response when a singer swung with "My Daddy Rocks Me With One Steady Roll": "My dear! Oh, my dear, how beautifully you sing spirituals."[19] This was in the swing era of the 1920s.

Joe Turner, one of the very first of the Kansas City Blues shouters, was the coauthor with Pete Johnson of "Cherry Red," a 1939 blues hit, and there is no question about the sexual reference made toward "rock."

> Take me pretty mama, chunk me in your big brass bed
> And rock me mama till my face turns Cherry Red.

In the late forties Jimmy Witherspoon, one of the real greats of rhythm and blues, recorded a hit song called "No Rollin' Blues."

> When you come home in the evening
> And everything you do is wrong
> You might as well pack your clothes and leave
> Cause somebody else is carrying your rollin' on.

Although "Cherry Red" and "No Rollin' Blues" were hit recordings, neither sold three million copies as did the 1951 secular quartet recording of "Sixty Minute Man" by the famous Dominos. The song was written by Billy Ward and Rosa Marks.

> Listen here girl I'm telling you now
> They call me loving Dan.
> I'll rock 'em and roll 'em all night long
> I'm a sixty minute man.

These are only a few examples of many songs which made a sexual reference to rocking, rolling, or both and most were before 1950. To an outsider, the sex reference may have been hidden because the words did not always indicate a sexual meaning. "Yeah! We're gonna rock this joint tonight" meant a musical happening. Sometimes the meaning wasn't exactly clear either: "Let it roll, let it roll, all night long, let it roll." Maybe "it" was music and good times, maybe not. The important factor is that rock and roll were significant African-American social expressions and can be observed as an intrinsic part of early rhythm and blues music.

The success of African work-gang structured groups, the Orioles and the Dominos, revealed, just as Perry Bradford and Mamie Smith had done decades earlier, a whole new vista for popular Afro-American music. And just as the phonograph was the factor in the twenties, radio by 1951 was the most significant agent. As Arnold Shaw author of *The World of Soul* has stated,

> I have become convinced that the role of Black radio and Black disk jockeys in the history of the blues has been grossly neglected. Because recordings are accessible long after they have been released, their impact on bluesmen has been stressed and overstressed. But cotton patch workers are not record collectors.[20]

Although the last statement can be argued, Shaw's intended point is clear, and our next chapter will discuss radio's impact upon rhythm and blues.

REFERENCES

1. Dorothy Scarborough, *On the Trail of Negro Folk Songs* (Cambridge, Mass.: Harvard University Press, 1925), p. 216.

2. LeRoi Jones, *The Blues People* (New York: William Morrow, 1963), p. 62.

3. W. C. Handy, *Father of the Blues* (New York: Macmillan and Company, 1941), p. 76.

4. Scarborough, op. cit., p. 265.

5. John Work, *American Negro Songs* (New York: Howell, Saskin and Company, 1940), p. 33.

6. Samuel Charters, *The Country Blues* (New York: Rinehart, 1959), p. 189.

7. Perry Bradford, *Born With the Blues* (New York: Oak Publications, 1965), p. 13.

8. Paul Oliver, *Blues Fell This Morning* (New York: Horizon Press, 1966), p. 1.

9. Charters, op. cit., p. 47.

10. Charles Keil, *The Urban Blues* (Chicago: The University of Chicago Press, 1966), p. 65.

11. Ibid., p. 63.

12. Raymond Horricks, *Count Basie and His Orchestra* (New York, The Citadel Press, 1957), p. 41.

13. Charters, op. cit., p. 238.

14. Keil, op. cit., p. 65.

15. Maud-Cuney Hare, *Negro Musicans and Their Music* (Washington, D. C.: Associated Publishers, 1936), p. 154.

16. *Billboard* Magazine, April 7, 1945, p. 2.

17. *Ebony* Magazine, September 1952, p. 26.

18. *Downbeat,* December 30, 1953, p. 3.

19. Langston Hughes, *The Big Sea* (New York: Alfred A. Knopf, 1940), p. 254.

20. Arnold Shaw, *The World of Soul* (New York: Cowles Book Company, 1970), p. x.

CHAPTER 2.

Radio

The Disc Jockey

THERE WERE NO RADIO STATIONS IN 1900. THE PHONOGRAPH WAS barely a concept and usually referred to as a "talking machine." Music, however, was an important part of American life. For the most part, African-Americans made their music from the soul, what they heard and memorized, and what they created in jam sessions. The formal music industry was, as it had always been in America, controlled by music publishing companies. At the turn of the century, if you wanted music you had to play it yourself or find someone else to perform it. The publisher sold sheet music to all who could read. That is where the money was. And that is still where a great deal of money is today. The publisher decided which songs deserved to be initially pushed and plugged.

In one sense, the major impact of radio on the music industry has been the transfer of this power from the publishers to the broadcasters, whether the publishers liked it or not. And they did not. When disc jockeys first appeared in the 1930s, as near as anyone seems capable of determining, some artists such as Bing Crosby and Fred Waring had their record labels include the warning "NOT LICENSED FOR RADIO BROADCAST." Far from welcoming the disc jockeys, the big name recording stars erected their own roadblocks. And for a time they had some success.

But in 1940 the litigation came to a debacle in a suit involving Paul Whiteman records. The court ruled that a broadcaster, having purchased a phonograph record, could broadcast it without further obligation, regardless of the wishes of artists or manufacturers. The warning on label was held to have no legal significance. The U. S. Supreme Court declined to review the case. The ruling put the disc jockey for the first time on secure legal footing.[1]

Of course, broadcasting stations paid the American Society of Composers, Authors, and Publishers fees for playing recorded music.

In 1941 ASCAP decided to increase broadcasting royalty rates. Broadcasting replied by temporarily banning all ASCAP material from the air. ASCAP withdrew its demands. The disc jockey had proved his ability not only to make sales for sponsors but also to increase record sales where market performance had been "killed" during the Depression. By 1935 disc jockeys had revived sales in both sheet and phonograph categories. By 1941 many music houses had long since phased out their piano player, whose job it had been to play newly released sheet music for customers. Without broadcasting as a mass catalyst to phonograph sales which spurred sheet music sales—ASCAP was hurting. The balance of power was shifting.

During the Depression networks and large stations remained profitable. However, in the post World War II period even the small stations enjoyed a financially profitable era. The disc jockey was on the scene with ad lib commercials and rip and read news from the AP or UP or INS news ticker service. The new image of radio in America was perhaps best described by J. Harold Ryan, who in 1945 was the newly elected president of NAB:

> American radio is the product of American business! It is just as much that kind of product as the vacuum cleaner, the washing machine, the automobile and the airplane. . . . If the legend still persists that a radio station is some kind of art center, a technical museum, or a little piece of Hollywood transplanted strangely to your home town, then the first official act of the second quarter century should be listing it along with the local dairies, laundries, banks, restaurants, and filling stations.[2]

After World War II, radio made every effort to achieve the goal Ryan mentioned. The networks began by hiring some of the top names in the show business world in an effort to successfully ride the bandwagon of the "disc jockey." Ted Husing, Paul Whiteman, Duke Ellington, Kate Smith, Deems Taylor, Mel Allen, Woody Herman, and Tommy Dorsey were signed at astonishingly high salaries to do disc jockey work back in 1946.[3] Arthur Treacher and Eddie Cantor also joined the ranks for awhile.

However, simply having a big name spin records was not enough to captivate radio audiences. Soon young unknowns working small independent stations began dominating the local and regional air waves. In short, they upset not only the broadcasting establishment, but, according to *Variety* magazine, the music world.

In the past couple of years the record promotion block has emerged as a key
factor in the new music business. Before the disk became "king" of Tin Pan
Alley, the publishers' contact men were solely responsible for the tune plugs,
but in today's wax age, the disk promotion man, operating on an indie basis,
has become the dominant plug force.

Disk promotion developed into a booming biz during the last five years as
artists realized that the disk jockey outlet was the main source of pop record
sales promotion at the consumer and juke level. As they began latching on
to disk promoters for personal service, an increasing number of flocks moved
into this field.

As one disk promoter put it—"we're to the record industry what an advertising agency is to any other biz."[4]

The new phonograph advertiser was not embraced by everyone in
the business. In the late forties and early fifties the disc jockey
became a controversial figure. He was praised by some and criticized
by others. Editorials appeared in music trade magazines both pro
and con. Old-timers, remembering the good old days, said disc jockeys had too much power, and they criticized the current music by
such people as Johnnie Ray and Ralph Flanagan. Music critic Nat
Hentoff sided with the old heads.

Our level of popular music has become so pitiful, not because of the public
primarily, but because of the recording directors, the song publishers, and,
especially, the disc jockeys.

Who is responsible for the musically unmerited success of more recent
tonal gargoyles like Johnnie Ray and stale dance bands of the depressing
caliber of Ralph Flanagan and Ray Anthony?

With a few highly commendable exceptions, the contemporary disc jockey
has reached a fantastic state of pompous musical ignorance and limitless
arrogance in the use of that ignorance. These grotesques would be laughable
except that they exercise tremendous power.

They decide what their listeners will hear, and don't let any of them tell
you it works the other way around. Look at these shabby "hits" manufactured
by incessant, relentless disc jockey plugging.[5]

"Payola" was the subject of grave concern almost the instant that
the disc jockey's popularity mushroomed after World War II. Some
people in the music business, the publishers to be specific, referred
to disc jockeys as the Frankenstein of the music industry. On the
other hand, others claimed that the disc jockey gave new talent a
break, that he weeded out the untalented female with a thirty-nine
inch bust who could not be seen via records, and that he gave the
independent record producer a fair shake. Those who sided with the

disc jockey claimed that payoffs could be stopped if the publishers themselves would cease the dollar stampede. At the height of the disc jockey dispute in 1951 a then well-known disc jockey who refused to be identified laid out the heart of the matter to *Variety:*

> There's no disputing the stature of the deejay and his affirmative contribution to the music business. . . . but the music publisher has lost control of his copyright which technically is owned by his publishing firm but which is theoretical because the recording company takes hold, and from then on the fate of the song, the songwriter and the publisher are in (a) the disk interpretation and (b) the disk jockey.[6]

Even beyond the arguments between music publishers and disc jockeys, lay the crux of the matter. Radio was opening the airways and giving people a choice of wider selectivity. Somebody had to win, or worse yet, lose. Noted music critic Ralph J. Gleason summed up post World War II this way:

> After World War II, radio changed under pressure from television to low budget music and news programs. The pop record business eagerly took over the AM air waves. City and country blues and hillbilly music were available on the air alongside the Broadway show tunes and popular ballads. For the first time young people had a truly free choice in what they wanted to listen to on the air.[7]

Generally, Broadway held its own through the late forties, and Hank Williams lifted country and western to its greatest popularity in the early fifties. James Denny, radio station manager of Nashville's WSM in 1954, accredited radio as a major influence in the popularity growth of country and western music.

> Primarily, four factors are responsible for the evolution: the creation of the singing star, a shift in national population, the growth of radio, and the decline in the quality of the popular music that flooded the country.[8]

Then the final music selection was made. The musical course which was to shape the world and future generations was extraneously agreed upon. At first the sound of rhythm and blues was like a soft drum, whose beat traveled great distances and faintly touched the ears of young pop radio listeners. It tickled and made noncreators laugh and joke about it. The music was an esoteric message that spoke only to its creators and the most aware nonmembers, who told their friends. To many of them the beat was funny, and they called it a passing fad. But the winds of rhythm grew stronger and louder; it touched the souls of young white Americans. They rocked and spun aboutface, embracing Africa's rhythmic beat. Their parents protested, calling the music vulgar, barren, and animalistic. But it was too late—there were no ships sailing for Africa.

By 1954 America was in the midst of a musical explosion. Abram Chasins, then music director of a New York radio station, WQXR, wrote an article for *Variety* claiming that radio had the major impact on modern music's popularity explosion.

> At this moment, the art of music has the largest audience ever assembled to hear it in the history of mankind . . . those responsible for the musical wealth of our country include composers, interpreters, inventors, publishers, recording companies, licensing agencies (whose protection encourages composers and facilitates the availability of their music to the user) an eager public, and to my mind, the most effective force the broadcasters.[9]

African-American Programing

Ironically, African-American music has a long, though thin, history in broadcasting. The first radio station in America, WWJ in Detroit, went on the air in 1920. In 1924 Bessie Smith appeared on Memphis radio station WMC:

> Bessie Smith, colored singer of deep indigo blues, gave WMC listeners a treat with a score of her latest successes as she led the midnight frolic at 11 o'clock last night, with Yancey and Booker's orchestra and the Beale Avenue Palace theater orchestra playing accompaniments in slow, negroid rhythm.
>
> "Sam Jones Blues," "Chicago Bound," "St. Louis Gal," and "Mistreatin' Pap" led the way for a score of others. Bessie has a voice that will never be mistaken for another's. She is in a class by herself in the field of "blues."
>
> The two orchestras, splitting the midnight frolic, were delightful in their original handling of the popular numbers of today. They took back the numbers written from the old Negro folk songs and put that Negro touch to them that the authors missed. The boys put Beale Avenue into the air, with the result that WMC was flooded with requests from the territory and was the recipient of wires from East, West, North, and South.[10]

Network programing using African-Americans was seemingly widespread by the early 1930s, when radio was mainly programing music. Black orchestras and singing groups were broadcast regularly, including a religious group called the Southernairs who came on every Sunday morning. However, when drama became popular and dominated the air waves, blacks were out. The sustaining thrust of black radio appears to have taken an initial form of local weekly programing on Sunday by gospel quartets. In 1941 *Time* Magazine carried an article on the famous Golden Gate Quartet, indicating they were broadcasting before 1935:

> Tenors Willie Langford and Henry Owen, Baritone Willie Johnson and Basso Orlandus Wilson began singing together in Norfolk, Virginia's Booker T. Washington High School, got on local radio programs even before they graduated in 1935.[11]

The Swan Silvertones, another famous gospel quartet also trace their roots back to radio in the 1930s. Moving from West Virginia in 1939 to Knoxville, Tennessee, they obtained a weekly Sunday morning radio show.[12]

Radio station WLAC, a 50,000-watt company in Nashville, Tennessee, began carrying religious recordings by black artists back in early 1946, sponsored by Randy Wood of Gallitin, Tennessee. The program became so popular among blacks, and has carried over so strongly, that even today many older African-Americans tend to refer to WLAC radio as Randy's.

Development of African-American Radio

Segmented local programing for blacks during the late thirties and early forties seems to have been widespread throughout southern United States. However, not until 1948 did full-time broadcasting to African-Americans come into being. Radio WDIA in Memphis, Tennessee, went on the air in 1947, aiming its programing toward whites. The first year it wound up in the red. The following year WDIA took full advantage of the kingpin position Memphis held as a rhythm and blues center and swung its 50,000 watts toward the one and a half million blacks in Tennessee, Arkansas, Missouri, and Mississippi. Black disc jockeys were already being heard in these states. Howlin Wolf, a famous blues singer, had for several years been a disc jockey on WKUM. Arnold Shaw in his book *The World of Soul* revealed that

Elmore James was a WOKI (Jackson, Mississippi) disc jockey. From 1938 intermittently for almost three decades the second Sonny Boy Williamson broadcast daily on "King Biscuit Time" over KFFA of Helena, Arkansas, and WROX of Clarksdale, Mississippi.[13]

Needless to say, over the years WDIA has remained in the black in more ways than one. But even more important was the trend toward full-time black radio that WDIA started. Radio stations aiming their programing toward blacks rapidly began springing up all across the Southland and in some cases up North—WJLD, Birmingham; WERD, Atlanta;KXLW, St. Louis; WMRY, New Orleans. By 1951 most large southern cities had black-oriented radio stations. The potential rhythm and blues explosion could no longer be halted.

As witnessed by the 1948 decision of WDIA, which has remained white-owned, development of black radio programing was not so much the result of love of African-American culture, but rather a source from which businessmen in radio could make money. In February 1953, *Variety* expounded upon the circumstances surrounding the widespread birth of black radio stations.

Strong upsurge in r and b [rhythm and blues] market in recent years has now put the Negro disc jockey into one of the key positions in the overall music business. Over 500 r and b jocks are now spotted on stations in every city where there is a sizable colored population.

The Negro jocks have come into their own in the key cities since the advent of video. TV has been forcing the indie radio outlet into specialized programing projects and the pitch to the vast Negro market is proving easiest via the platter spinning route.

The Negro disk jockey has a much stronger standing in the colored community, particularly in the South, than the ofay platter pilots have generally due to the social situation. This influence over their listeners is proportionately stronger and that explains why their shows are solid commercial stanzas.

Their accent on r and b platters stems from that music's widespread and almost unique acceptance by Negro audiences.[14]

The South had long preceded the North in opening up broadcasting to blacks. By 1953 black disc jockeys worked throughout the country.

New York metropolitan area has one of the largest concentrations of Negro jocks in the country with twelve now on the air. These are: Jack Walker WOU, Joe Bostic WBNX, Willie Bryant WHOM-WOR, Hal Jackson

WMCA, Phil Gordon WLIB, Tommy Small WWRL, Howard Bowser and Sarah Lou WLIB, Lucky Millinder WNEW, Doc Wheeler WWRL, Larry Fuller WLIB, and Bill Cook WAAT, Newark. Most of these jocks are on foreign language stations but have developed a strong enough hold to get their listeners to tune in at specific hours.

In Chicago Al Benson, on WGES and WJJD, is influential, while in the South there are numerous important deejays, including Vernon Winslow and Jack L. Cooper, in New Orleans; Sugar Daddy, in Birmingham; Bruce Miller, in Winston-Salem, North Carolina; Nat D. Williams, in Memphis; Jacqueline De Shazar, in Durham, North Carolina, and Jan Massey, in Washington, D. C.

Paradoxically, one of the most potent of the r and b deejays is Gene Nobles, a white jock who operates out of Gallatin, Tennessee. Nobles has developed a nationwide following via his WLAC stanzas for Randy Wood's platter mail-order operation and his r and b label, Dot Records.[15]

Much debate has gone into tracing the exact record which is supposed to have started the rock revolution. Such a search could theoretically lead back to the nineteenth century days of Thomas Rice and the minstrel show, for white Americans have always kept a finger on the pulse of black entertainment. It should be clear by now that no such record "really" exists. The explosion of rhythm and blues did not rest on one record. Rather, the impact of radio and the rhythm and blues disc jockeys were the major causes of the music's widespread outburst of popularity in the late forties and early fifties.

Through radio, Elvis Presley, obtained a valuable portion of his background in rhythm and blues. WDIA became a friend to Presley, according to writer Robert Blair Kaiser, whenever self-doubts troubled the Memphian.

He would go off by himself to thrum a $2.50 guitar and sing the songs of the people—the soul music of the hills—or just listen to the blues being aired then on the black station in Memphis, WDIA. That music was too earthy, too sexy for nice white folks. But Elvis listened, to Arthur (Big Boy) Crudup and Kokomo Arnold and Arthur Gunter and Little Junior Parker and Chuck Willis, and later, when he started recording—mainly "country" stuff at first—for Sam Phillips at Sun Records, he cut his idols' music on the flip sides.[16]

Presley was a microcosm of other white youths who learned to appreciate the sound of rhythm and blues via the medium of radio broadcasting. "Once records were on the air, everybody could hear them. . . . And it is certainly true that the current rage for r and b followed the exposure of the music on the radio."[17]

Discovery of Rhythm and Blues by Alan Freed

By the time Alan Freed got into the wonderful world of color, rhythm and blues was well developed. Black disc jockeys such as Nat Williams and Rufus Thomas of WDIA had established their rhythmic rhyming delivery, slipping tidbits in between swinging lyrics and talking back to records or artists as they performed their songs. By his own admission in *Downbeat,* Freed, who stumbled upon rhythm and blues by chance, found an exciting culture to draw from.

> It was in 1951. I had a program on WJW, a Cleveland station. The program music, believe it or not, was classical. A friend who owned a record shop suggested that I visit the store. He said I might see something unusual. I accepted the invitation and had one of the most thrilling experiences of my life. There were dozens of kids having a wonderful time listening to records of some of the people who were destined to become the very top performers in the idiom. . . .
>
> I listened. I heard the songs of such artists as La Verne Baker and Della Reese, two girls with real contralto voices who know how to tell a story. I heard the tenor saxophones of Red Prysock and Big Al Sears. I heard the blues-singing, piano-playing Ivory Joe Hunter. I wondered.
>
> I WONDERED for about a week. Then I went to the station manager and talked him into permitting me to follow my classical program with a rock 'n' roll party.[18]

Like WDIA and other stations in the South, the northern black community was delighted with their own musical culture being aired on radio. But in the North a different element entered the radio picture. Young whites were not discouraged from listening. Freed was white, and there was no previous taboo reference to the music. Freed decided to bring in some rhythm and blues stars for a small dance. To his amazement 25,000 people showed. Available data indicates his promotion was mainly via his radio program. People in the music business began to take a more serious look at the already emerging popularity of rhythm and blues.

Throughout the country, record stores at the request of young white buyers had already started selling rhythm and blues where none had been sold before. Juke box operators began reporting requests for rhythm and blues tunes from pop locations which heretofore detested the music as lowdown and noisy. Because pop record stores began including rhythm and blues in their sales, the tunes began showing up on local pop charts, and many pop radio stations, which would by today's references be called middle of the road, began playing a rhythm and blues song here and there. Jerry Flatts, owner of Boston Record Distributors, related the phenomenon to *Variety* in February 1954 in the wake of a big hit by the late Roy Hamilton called "You'll Never Walk Alone":

Rhythm and blues currently comprise about 10% of his sales—mostly to juke boxes—compared to less than 2% a year ago. His overall sales (in this category) show a jump of about 80%, and continue to build as juke box operators install the disks in locations that previously catered to strictly pop trade.

Credit for awakened interest in this type disk is three-fold—the airshows of D.J.'s Symphony Sid and Art Tucker, the all out peddling job of rhythm and blues labels, and Flatts' staff, who plug the records to juke box operators.[19]

Rhythm and blues record company owners took advantage of the potential expansion of their business and carefully aimed some of their artists for the pop markets via radio.

More of rhythm and blues output into the pop market is continuing to gain momentum. . . . Additional reports also point to an upbeat in the use of rhythm and blues platters by various D.J.'s who've been devoting their spins to pop releases.

Several recording groups that were previously confined to the rhythm and blues market have broken out with tunes that have made both the rhythm and blues and pop listings. Among these are the Orioles and the Four Tunes. The former group expanded into the pop field with their etching of "Crying in the Chapel," and have since been selling in the pop and rhythm and blues markets, while the latter combo is currently riding high pop-wise with *Marie*.

Another outfit marking a strong bid for pop market acceptance is the Dominos, who've recorded several standards including "These Foolish Things" and "Till the Real Thing Comes Along." Also falling in line with rhythm and blues in roads to pop field was Buddy Morris' recent acquisition of the tune, "Gee." The number was picked up by the pubbery following its recording by the Crows on the Rama label.[20]

The pop field was controlled almost exclusively by major record companies such as Capitol, Columbia, and Decca. The rhythm and blues companies were in most cases small independent labels such as Aladdin, Black and White, Atlantic, Duke, and Jubilee. The larger companies began to combat what they felt was an intrusion into the pop field money patch by the smaller companies with black artists. As soon as a rhythm and blues record started to take off, the larger companies would release a white artist singing the same song with the nearest arrangement possible to the rhythm and blues recording. Covering was an old trick used by large record companies dating back at least to 1947 with the Rhythm and Blues song "Open the Door Richard," which was based on an old black vaudeville act by the late Dusty Fletcher. *Time* magazine carried a story on it back in 1947:

> Last week another one of those catchy tunes and goofy phrases fairly leapt across the nation. Every radio blared *Open the Door, Richard!* Five record versions were on sale, and thirteen more (by Louis Jordan, Dick Haymes, the Pied Pipers, etc.) were being rushed to market. A quartet known as The Yokels sang it in Yiddish. Bing Crosby (an accessory after the fact), Bob Hope, Fred Allen and Bea Lillie had only to mention the word Richard on the air to put their studio audiences in stitches.[21]

Again in early 1953 *Variety* noted that the pop field was covering, or copying, rhythm and blues songs. *Variety* identified the musical source and unobtrusively pinpointed the rhythm and blues covering practice in its very early stages.

> The music stems from the jazz blues and the idiom of the lyrics uses the specialized jargon of the restricted Negro community. As a result, the 100% rhythm and blues platters sell only in the colored market although diluted interpretations have been seeping into the pop field with increasing frequency.[22]

A year and a half later the trade magazine did another article on the widening practice of covering rhythm and blues records. Although several covers of rhythm and blues appeared on the charts in 1954, one song carried almost as much fervor as "Open the Door Richard." It was from the Atlantic Record Company production staff. Rhythm and blues radio stations played the original "Sha-boom" by the Cords, and pop stations picked up the cover which was done by the Crew-Cuts. Rhythm and blues hit yet another plateau:

> Since the click of "Sha-boom" a flock of tunes have hit the market with nonsense titles. . . . All of these tunes have originated from the rhythm and blues field and the titles are based on vocal phrases used by singing combos.
>
> Current trend also spotlights once again the strength of rhythm and blues tunes into the general pop market. "Sha-boom" was originally written and sliced by a rhythm and blues outfit, the Chords, for the Cat label and was turned into a pop hit by the Crew-Cuts for Mercury.

Patti Page, also on Mercury followed Ruth Brown's "O' What a Dream" side for Atlantic and the McGuire Sisters picked up a rhythm and blues number, "Goodnight, Sweetheart, Goodnight," and turned it into a pop hit. To a large extent the invasion of the rhythm and blues tunes has virtually driven the hillbilly numbers out of the pop field.[23]

The latter statement becomes significantly important later in this chapter when rhythm and blues lyrics are discussed.

In most instances the cover concept worked, and white oriented stations began playing the pop artists singing rhythm and blues songs, which in many cases zoomed to the top of the pop charts ahead of original rhythm and blues recordings.

Covers kept most rhythm and blues artists at bay for awhile. Pop artists had found a new thing. And since blacks, then as now, influenced very little control of radio or record companies, all they could do was check out the action. Rhythm and blues popularity however, continued to spread and mushroom. And out in the Midwest Alan Freed continued to increase rhythm and blues action with more successful package "star" shows.

In 1954 WINS radio station became interested in bringing Freed to New York as a full-time jockey to do his thing. Contrary to popular beliefs, Freed did not instantly begin referring to rhythm and blues as rock and roll once he put it on WJW in Cleveland. In the style of black disc jockeys, he gave himself a nickname—Moondog. King of the Moondoggers, he called himself. The rhythm and blues shows were known as Moondog shows, and his audience as Moondoggers. However, according to *Downbeat* when Freed arrived in New York, another Moondog was already on the scene, and he took Freed to court.

"The first Moondog" the Blind Broadway street musician who plays complex rhythmic percussion compositions in doorways and on recordings [Coral and Epic LP: Real name Louis Hardin].

The second is a rhythm and blues disc jockey from Cleveland who will soon move onto WINS, New York. He not only calls himself Moondog but produces successful Moondog Balls starring rhythm and blues artists. His real name is Alan Freed.

The suit asks that the disc jockey be injoined from further use of the name and asks for damages.[24]

Hardin won the court case, and Freed was left without the gimmick name which had helped to attract so many black people back in Ohio. Freed had a trump card, he rationalized that if he called the music rock and roll, a recurring phrase in rhythm and blues songs, it would broaden the popularity of the music by making it even more acceptable to young whites.

Downbeat captured the birth of the rhythm and blues dichotomy that radio and Alan Freed had created:

> Moondog [Hardin, L.] has won the court fight to prevent rhythm and blues disc jockey Alan Freed [WINS] from using the "Moondog" title. Freed, complying with the injunction, now calls his program the Rock and Roll Show.
>
> Freed meanwhile has achieved major audience impact in the New York area and will present his first rhythm and blues dance here January 14 and 15 at the St. Nicholas Arena. Freed's radio show is also growing in the number of cities it reaches. The syndicated program has been set for Kansas City, St. Louis, New Orleans, Jackson, Mississippi, and Flint, Michigan, with five other southern markets in the offing.[25]

The power and impact of radio upon the growth and development of rhythm and blues flexed its strongest muscles when Freed took over the prime times slot at WINS. Leroy Carr said it best in the thirties with a song entitled "The Night Time Is the Right Time." Freed turned New York upside down with his evening rhythm and blues program. Though no less than twelve African-Americans had shows, young whites were free to identify with Freed, who was also white, even though the music was black.

When Freed called rhythm and blues "rock and roll," to whites who had never before heard rhythm and blues, it was as if rock and roll had no past, only a present reference. And indeed most of them were hearing rhythm and blues for the first time. Just as Africans brought to America were renamed Negroes and thus cut off from a glorious heritage, the reference to rhythm and blues as rock and roll created a similarly confusing parallel. As both Africans and Negroes existed separately in the mind of America, so rhythm and blues and rock and roll were also divided.

It must be remembered that New York City in 1954, was as it is today, the show business capital of the nation. Whatever happened there soon became the vogue elsewhere. Therefore, if New York said rhythm and blues is now changing its name to rock and roll, the rest of the nation agreed because New York was vogue and because Alan Freed controlled the music popularity scene in New York. According to Herman Schoenfield:

The big beat in the pop music biz these days is rhythm and blues and the top
name in the rhythm and blues field today is Allen Freed, the rock 'n' roll disk
jockey who recently moved from Cleveland to WINS in New York, where
he has become a major factor in metropolitan night time radio. Once limited
to the Negro market, the rhythm and blues influence has now crossed all color
lines into the general pop market.[26]

It was Christmas out of season for rhythm and blues; everybody
seemed to embrace the African-American music.

Booking dates for rhythm and blues artists began to increase
significantly. *Billboard* carried a story which indicated radio was
primarily involved in the new upsurge of rhythm and blues.

The big news in the rhythm and blues personal appearance field for 1955 was
the emergence of the deejay as a powerhouse promoter. At the same time,
agencies happily noted an increase of niteries booking rhythm and blues
talent, and prosperity continued in the one-night field.[27]

Freed was, however, only a part of a much larger rhythm and
blues picture. As far back as the late forties when Nat Williams,
Rufus Thomas, and others were making WDIA a successful black-
oriented broadcasting station, they had used the "package show"
idea with the charity Star-Lite Revue in the summer and Goodwill
Revue in the fall. And in New York, prior to Freed's arrival Tommy
Small, WWRL, had brought package rhythm and blues shows into
Harlem's Apollo Theater. Freed's side of the society was, however,
much larger; and with shrewd promotion and mass attention being
given rhythm and blues, the package shows, as a sign of rhythm and
blues popularity, became bigger than ever.

And Freed, reported *Billboard,* was into the money:

His first show last spring at the Brooklyn Paramount grossed the all-time
house record of $125,000, while his second show at the same theatre later that
year piled up another record-breaking gross of $155,000, and his Christmas
weekend bill at the Academy Theatre, New York, pulled in another $125,-
000.[28]

Whether a rhythm and blues fan caught an Alan Freed show or
a Tommy "Mr. Jive" Small show, the excitement was always genuine. The stars, pioneers of music revolution, were a who's who of now
forgotten but great contributors to the now sound of the what's
happening generation of today. Roy Hamilton shook the music scene
with "You'll Never Walk Alone" and later with a follow-up "Un-
chained Melody." Bo Diddly was working with "I'm a Man". Fats

Domino, who had been on the rhythm and blues charts since 1950, rocked everybody with "Ain't It A Shame." Joe Turner, the man from Kansas who started male vocal blues swinging in front of heavy rhythmic jazz bands, gained tremendous success with "Shake, Rattle, and Roll." The Clovers made the charts with the unforgettable "Lovey Dovey." and the sweet tender sound of the Spaniels' "Goodnight Sweetheart" echoed across auditoriums and shacks unprepared for the rhythm and blues explosion. The Five Royals pleaded "Help Me Somebody"; Faye Adams answered "Shake a Hand"; and the Cardinals lamented "The Door Is Still Open."

Rhythm and blues, influenced by powerful radio network programing and WINS with Alan Freed, was now being referred to by many as rock and roll. Despite the semantic differential, rhythm and blues artists met the challenge of increased popularity demand. Ruth Cage, writing for *Downbeat,* captured every movement of the rhythm and blues explosion.

> Working thirty-two days straight may be viewed as a harrowing experience even under sedentary conditions.—Despite such a schedule though, a bunch of rhythm and blues stars seem not too unhappy these days—the reasons probably are loot and fantastic public acceptance.[29]

The tremendous popularity spread of the music was not to be denied very long among any faction in the music or broadcasting industry. When the dust finally settled on 1954, *Billboard* discovered that rhythm and blues songs and artists had captured eight of the top twenty-five best-selling positions in the pop market. The 1955 picture was even better:

> But for an overall look at the phenomenon, illuminating insight is provided by a rundown of tunes, which won awards from Broadcast Music, Inc., for heavy action during 1955. Of the twenty-eight awards given out by the licensing organization, no less than sixteen were rhythm and blues derived.
>
> Arc Music, a publishing operation involving the principals of Chess and Checker Records, had "Maybellene" and "Sincerely"; Lois Music, an affiliate of Kind and De Luxe, won with "Rock Love" and "Seventeen"; Progressive Music, the publishing arm of Atlantic Records, placed with "Tweedle Dee"; Savoy Music, an affiliate of the diskery bearing the same name, had "Don't Be Angry" in partnership with Republic Music.
>
> Also, Lion Publishing (Peacock and Duke Records) won an award with "Pledging My Love," Dootsie Williams Publications (Dootone Records) with "Earth Angel," Tollie Music (Vee Jay Records) with "At My Front Door,"

Commodore Music (Imperial Records) with "Ain't That a Shame?" and "I Hear You Knockin" and Modern Music (Modern and RPM Records) with "Dance with Me Henry."[30]

From a social perspective the breakthrough of rhythm and blues into the pop market represented a most significant precedent in the American society. The record industry segregated the music in the 1920s by clearly labeling African-American music, "race" music. That racist tradition was being reversed, and young white Americans of the 1950s turned the tide in America. Radio was the vehicle through which most of them discovered the African-American music.

After 1955 it became apparent to the power structure of the music world that rhythm and blues was not going to retreat from its newly conquered territory. In February 1956 *Billboard,* in an editorial, officially welcomed rhythm and blues into the mainstream of American heritage:

One of the most meaningful developments in years on the music-record scene has been the mass acceptance of rhythm and blues—its emergence from narrow confines and its impact on the broad field of pop music. The past year has been crucial in this development. During 1955 it became apparent that notwithstanding the opposition of entrenched facets of the music business, this exciting form of musical expression, together with its notable body of artists, could not longer be relegated to a relatively unimportant niche.

In the last analysis, it was, of course, the kid with the 89 cents in his pocket who cast the deciding vote. He considered the repertoire, listened to the imaginative arrangements of the artists and repertoire men, critically weighed the merits of the artists—and found them all good.

We have, in the singles business, a mass of repertoire and artists, writers and arrangers whose output is a constant spur to virtually the entire field. Recapitulations of the top tunes of the year, the top records of the year, the top publishers of the year—all of them carried recently in *The Billboard*—bear out the one theme: Namely, this is rhythm and blues' greatest era. The idiom has come along with such overwhelming force as to leave no doubt of its validity as a major contribution to the American musical scene.

The record business thrives on excitement, on action. It is our earnest hope that rhythm and blues shall never lose its brightness; may the well-spring of talent never dry up; may the aggressive labels, distributors and dealers never lose their magic touch since many benefits have accrued from rhythm and blues' coming of age. For the artists in the field it has meant artistic fulfillment and economic well-being. Much the same may be said of the a & r men, arrangers, distributors and dealers—all of whom never lost faith. For the pop field, or let us say for those in the pop field who were sharp enough to recognize the full significance of the impact, it meant an infusion of brightness and excitement which did the singles business much good at the consumer and artistic levels.

The horizons for rhythm and blues have never been broader, the aspect never sunnier. From the mass point of view, it is no longer in the category of the unproved. It is impossible to forecast all the vagaries of public taste, but it would seem to us that talent coupled with belief in one's product is a well-nigh unbeatable combination. Let the field go forward on this basis. And, of course, let us not forget the kid with the 89 cents.[31]

Whatever will eventually be written about Alan Freed, he was prophetic in 1954 concerning the broad acceptance of rhythm and blues on his show by referring to the music as rock and roll. It is doubtful that Freed was attempting to create a dichotomy within the music or that he anticipated the tremendous impact New York City radio would have upon the rest of the nation. Certainly other important variables such as record company promotion had its impact upon the music of black America, but the phrase rock and roll, taken from rhythm and blues song lyrics certainly had a magic attraction to young white Americans in the mid-fifties, and it all started on radio.

Rhythm and Blues Criticism

The popularity of rhythm and blues was not, of course, welcomed pervasively in America. In some instances it was not so much a dislike for rhythm and blues music as a protection of vested interests. Broadcast Music Incorporated licensed most rhythm and blues music which was taking the country by storm, and the American Society of Composers, Authors, and Publishers may have been stabilizing their hit songs by raising some questions about rhythm and blues lyrics.

This also appears to be somewhat the situation surrounding rhythm and blues and country and western music. Country and western music emerged on the pop market scene in the late forties and early fifties and maintained a steady increase of popularity until rhythm and blues seemingly overshadowed it in the mid-fifties. Not only did rhythm and blues have an impact upon the pop market, but Ben Grevatt, writing for *Billboard,* indicated that black music also caused considerable influence *again* in the country and western field:

While this acceptance in the pop field shows no signs of diminishing it is also noteworthy that rhythm and blues is having an increasing impact on the country and western field. Here, an increasing amount of sides are being cut using rhythm and blues-flavored material. Much of it is in the blues category and in a sense this goes back to an older country and western era when much of the repertoire was in the nature of folk blues. Jimmie Rogers was typical of this period, and country singers have never lost the touch.[32]

It cannot be accurately determined whether ASCAP or any country and western persons initiated the crusade against rhythm and blues. However, there is evidence which suggests some people in country and western music felt threatened by the emergence of rhythm and blues popularity which had overshadowed the popularity that country and western music had increasingly attained since 1950.

Randy Blake, a Chicago disc jockey on WJJD in 1955, did not appreciate the new influence of rock and roll upon country and western music. In January of that year *Downbeat* printed an article written by Blake who warned country and western radio to keep their business pure and stop the panic to rhythm and blues music:

True, there had been an increase in sales in the rhythm and blues field. But the same things had happened before, only in other fields—for instance, in the country music field following the advent of *Tennessee Waltz*. When that happened, did the rhythm and blues people attempt to turn out a bevy of Hank Williamses? No. Why? Simply because they had better sense.

All the time country music enjoyed its greatest period of prosperity, those in the rhythm and blues field went right along in their own department, catering to their own audience, attempting to increase their own benefits by turning out a better product *for persons who wanted rhythm and blues.* A sound policy that paid off.

But when the recent rhythm and blues increase came, all too many in the country music business readily abandoned their own field in an attempt to jump on the other fellow's bandwagon. Suddenly we were deluged with records by country music artists that were not country music—gosh-awful, brazen attempts at something these artists can't do and never will be able to do.[33]

The increase of this trend continued, however, and although the majority of country and western jockeys did not want to play rhythm and blues flavored songs by country artists they responded to them if they were requested. This widespread rhythm and blues characteristic in country and western music coupled with rhythm and blues euphemism—rock and roll led many people to conclude inaccurately that rock and roll was formed with a combination of pop, rhythm and blues, and country and western. It simply was not true. Country and western artists were capable of performing rhythm and blues due to the strong influence of country blues upon country and western music.

The country and western reaction to lyrics, which first appeared during the 1954 country and western disk jockeys' convention, only foreshadowed the end of the honeymoon popularity novelty of rock and roll. The lyrics of rhythm and blues songs were challenged as unfit for air play. This campaign initially appeared to be the death of rock and roll, but it only helped rhythm and blues check its questionable cultural expressions and broaden its toe-hold.

The number one rhythm and blues song in June 1954 was "Work with Me Annie" by the Midnighters. It left the music wide open for criticism:

Work with me Annie and get it While the gettin' is good, so good.

The group was led by Hank Ballard, the author of the song who later wrote "The Twist." It used, as all black groups did, the African worksong method of call and response between the leader and the workers. As the leader pleaded with Annie to work, the group pretended to respond as Annie.

LEADER: Work with me Annie.
GROUP: Uh ummm, uh ummm.
LEADER: Work with me Annie.
GROUP: Uh ummm, uh ummm.
LEADER: Work with me Annie
        And get while the gettin' is good.
GROUP: So good, so good, so good.

As one black historian once said, "Everything went on in that cabin; life, death, and all that's in between." Whether the reader agrees or not, "Work with Me Annie" is valid. Radio, however, did not consider it so or at least acceptable. Though it is unfair to say the Midnighters caused the attack on rhythm and blues lyrics, it is safe to conclude they did not help the situation at all. And if "Work with Me Annie" did not serve as a target, "Sexy Ways" by the

Midnighters is a sure winner. No lyrics are essential to demonstrate the waves of panic even the title must have caused back in the winter of 1954–55.

By March 1955 the attack on rhythm and blues lyrics was in high gear. Once again radio was at the center of the situation. *Variety,* and other trade magazines, carried articles attacking rhythm and blues:

> The most astonishing thing about the current craze for rhythm and blues records and their accompaning leer-ics is that it was ever permitted to happen.
>
> Their leerical concoctions belong in the more dimlit honkytonks and should never be heard on the air.
>
> The responsibility for this state of affairs must fall on the recording company which permits its business to be fouled by marketing filth. It also falls equally heavily on the D.J. who is actually the liaison or link between the record company and the public.[34]

> Between 40% and 50% of rhythm and blues disks submitted make the trash basket. That's according to two of Mobile's leading disk jocks. "Filth in both title and words makes their destruction a must," says Happy Wainwright, Night Prowler on station WARG.[35]
>
> A war between N. Y. radio indie WINS and Bob Haymes, songwriter and WCBS deejay, has ended in the "unofficial" banning of Haymes' composition on WINS. WINS' Chieftain Bob Leder accused Haymes of making wanton and capricious attacks about teen-agers who listen to rhythm and blues which is a favored brand of music on the radio indie.
>
> Haymes also stated he received about one hundred of what he called drop dead letters from listeners of Alan "Rock n' Roll" Freed, Chief WINS rhythm and blues exponent.[36]

One letter was written to Nick Kenny of the *New York Daily Mirror* and it called rhythm and blues:

> . . . poor music, badly recorded, with lyrics that are at best in poor taste . . . and at worst obscene . . . this trend in music (and I apologize for calling it music) is affecting the ideas and the lives of our children.[37]

Freed read the letter over the air. The attack on rhythm and blues was nationwide, and on the West Coast the action was just as hot and intense:

> Zeke Manners, KFWB, Hollywood disc jockey who broke into print recently, after taking a verbal swing at Peter Potter's anti-stand on rhythm and blues records, is being shunned in the same issue by the seventy other deejays working this area.

Manners sent out letters to fellow jocks: "It is my idea that the poor material can be weeded out and discarded, thus leaving a place for good rhythm and blues records which could be broadcast for the pleasure of those who enjoy this type of music."[38]

Zeke Manners received no replies.

Rhythm and blues lyrics via radio were ahead of their time by at least a decade. Today the lyrics of the questionable rhythm and blues songs would probably not be noticed as unusual. Sex in the mid-fifties was expressed simply as African-Americans chose to tell it; but African-American culture simply overwhelmed many white Americans of the larger society.

However, some people in the music business made objective observations about the overpublicized lyrics. Rhythm and blues was, of course, the initial target of raw lyrics, but once the finger was pointed at rhythm and blues lyrics, the entire music industry, including music critic Abel Green, found itself looking seriously at the lyrics that radio had been broadcasting for years within the dominant white culture.

If nothing else is accomplished, at least the music business has been made aware of the leer-ics.

Actually, the object of all leer-ists . . . has always been to get as close to the Main Object as possible, without stating it and or cleaning it up by marrying 'em off in the last line. The current crop of rock n' rollers is not beating around the bush, but without condoning 'em, it's at least a less hypocritical approach.

Maybe it is coincidence that Cole Porter's "All of You" plug song, out of his new smash "Silk Stockings" is now heard over the radio as "the sweet and pure of you" instead of its original "I'd like to take a tour of you (the north and south of you)." Even as ethereal an ode as Hammerstein's "All the Things You Are" ("that moment divine when all the things you are, are mine") is refined "All of you."[39]

In retrospect, perhaps the funniest outgrowth of rhythm and blues (rock and roll) criticism was the banning action proposed by the white Citizens Council in 1956:

Asa E. (Ace) Carter, self-appointed leader of the North Alabama Citizens Council, said last week that "bebop," "rock and roll," and all "Negro music" are designed to force "Negro culture" on the South. "Individual councils have formed action committees to call on owners of establishments with rock and roll music on their juke boxes," he said. "We also intend to see the people who sponsor the music, and the people who promote Negro bands for teen-agers." Rock and roll music, he said, "is the basic heavy beat of Negroes. It appeals to the very base of man, brings out the base in man, brings out the animalism and vulgarity."[40]

The attention drawn to rhythm and blues lyrics being broadcast over radio, and initiated as an instrument of death to rhythm and blues, actually served to compromise that small area of African-American expression which the larger society found unacceptable at the time and made the music universally compatible. As far back as 1954 the late Chuck Willis, a brilliant African-American songwriter, stated cleaner lyrics as one of the key reasons for the rise in the popularity of rhythm and blues: "With popularity has naturally come profit, and reputable companies don't have to trade on off-beat sex to pay the rent."[41]

Virtually every radio station playing rhythm and blues (rock and roll) records made efforts to ease the heat of bad publicity. Many stations banned the music. More important, however, was the result of radio's pressure on record companies and publishers to regulate themselves and eventually set codes for music intended for air use.

In Boston, Sherm Feller of WVDA headed a group of area disc jockeys in drawing up a code to regulate the airing of records aimed at eliminating the lyric problem and widespread unfavorable publicity.

Critic Abel Green discovered that BMI was "undertaking a screening process," as close to the source as possible in an attempt to halt unfavorable lyrics via a team of three representative-intra company groups of five, or fifteen in all. As Abel saw it, some very important questions needed answering:

Whose responsibility is what? Where shall there be control in the rhythm and blues stuff. What yardstick of measurement should apply? If recorded, allegedly for some consumption does it perforce mean it shouldn't be broadcast? Is a daytime deejay's programing uniform with the type of stuff a post-midnight deejay broadcasts?[42]

Though it may appear through historical records that trade magazines were attacking rhythm and blues lyrics, African-American disc jockeys apparently appreciated the public airing of the issue. *Downbeat* covered their historic meeting of August 1956.

National Jazz and Rhythm and Blues D.J.'s Association convened at Small's Paradise in Harlem in August. Tommy Smalls of WWRL was host. D.J.'s adopted a code of operation and "went on record with a vote of thanks to the

trade publications for helping counteract the bad publicity received by
Rhythm and Blues music. . . ."[43]

Radio brought rhythm and blues within reach of a greater segment
of the public than had ever been dreamed possible by those who
pioneered the music. Though radio exposed and helped prepare
rhythm and blues as the music conqueror of the free world under the
euphemism of rock and roll, two other media also significantly made
their impact upon the music—motion pictures and television.

REFERENCES

1. Erik Barnouw, *A History of Broadcasting in the United States* (New York: Oxford University Press, 1968), p. 217.

2. Charles Siepmann, *Radio's Second Chance* (Boston: Little, Brown, and Company, 1946), p. 186.

3. Andre Baruch, *Variety,* Vol. 173 (January 5, 1949), p. 173.

4. D.J.'s Key Factor," *Variety,* Vol. 190 (April 29, 1953), p. 51.

5. Nat Hentoff, *Downbeat,* March 21, 1952, p. 1.

6. *Variety,* August 3, 1951, p. 41.

7. Ralph Gleason, *The Young Americans* (New York: Time Inc., 1966), p. 68.

8. *Downbeat,* Vol. 21 (June 30, 1954), p. 66.

9. Abram Chasins, "U. S. Coming of Age on Music: Radio a Big Factor," *Variety,* Vol. 196 (October 20, 1954), p. 51.

10. Columbia LP 33.

11. *Time,* January 29, 1941, p. 50.

12. Exodus LP 58, Spiritual Series.

13. Shaw, *op. cit.,* p. x.

14. *Variety,* Vol. 189 (February 25, 1953), p. 39.

15. *Variety,* Vol. 189 (February 25, 1953), p. 46.

16. Robert Kaiser, "The Rediscovery of Elvis," *New York Times Magazine,* October 11, 1970, p. 47.

17. Lindsay Patterson, ed., International Library of Negro Life and History, *The Negro in Music and Art* (New York: Publishers Company Inc., 1968), p. 117.

18. Alan Freed, "I Told You So," *Downbeat,* Vol. 23 (September 19, 1956), p. 44.

19. *Variety,* Vol. 193 (February 10, 1954), p. 58.

20. *Ibid.,* p. 51.

21. *Time,* Vol. 49 (February 10, 1947), p. 42.

22. *Variety,* Vol. 189 (February 25, 1953), p. 46.

23. *Variety,* Vol. 196 (September 22, 1954), p. 43.

24. Ruth Cage, "Rhythm and Blues," *Downbeat,* Vol. 21 (August 25, 1954), p. 17.

25. *Downbeat,* Vol.22 (January 12, 1955), p. 2.

26. Herman Schoenfield, *Variety,* Vol. 197 (January 19, 1955), p. 49.

27. *Billboard,* Vol. 66 (February 4, 1956), p. 48.

28. *Ibid.,* p. 48.

29. Ruth Cage, *Downbeat,* Vol. 22 (March 9, 1954), p. 9.

30. "Rhythm and Blues Spreads Wing," *Billboard,* Vol. 68 (February 4, 1956), p. 55.

31. *Ibid.,* p. 54.

32. Ben Grevatt, *Billboard,* Vol. 68 (February 4, 1956), p. 54.

33. Randy Blake, "Disc Jockey Urges Return to Spinning Only Country Music," *Downbeat,* Vol. 22 (January 26, 1955), p. 19.

34. Jimmy Kennedy, *Variety,* Vol. 198 (March 9, 1955), p. 49.

35. *Variety,* Vol. 198 (March 30, 1955), p. 54.

36. *Variety,* March 9, 1955, p. 44.

37. *Ibid.*

38. *Variety,* March 30, 1955, p. 54.

39. *Variety,* March 9, 1955, p. 49.

40. *Newsweek,* April 23, 1956, p. 32.

41. "Blues Getting Cleaner," *Downbeat,* Vol. 21 (November 3, 1954), p. 21.

42. Abel Green, *Variety,* March 9, 1955, p. 49.

43. *Downbeat,* September 19, 1956, p. 20.

CHAPTER 3.

Motion Pictures

Louis Jordan
and Early Rhythm and Blues Films

WORLD WAR II BROUGHT MANY BLACK MUSICIANS TOGETHER, and the music they played overseas attracted the attention of some important people. One group of black soldiers fighting in the South Pacific formed a group called the Jungle Band. They were so popular that the mayor of San Francisco turned the entire city out to greet them on their arrival home after the war, and for a brief period a fad existed for camouflaged "jungle suits." Few bands, if any, however, surpassed the popularity of the stateside band of Louis Jordan and the Tympany Five. In the mid-1940s Jordan, a saxophonist, was perhaps the most popular black entertainer in America. Not only did he toot a mean sax, he danced, sang, and cracked jokes. All of this led to Jordan's immortality on the silver screen.

For twenty-five years a few small independent motion picture producers, with studios in New York, Chicago, and Dallas, had attempted to corner the African-American market. Far removed from Hollywood, their shoestring production budgets, ranging from $40,000 to $60,000 per picture, mostly musicals, captured the new rhythmic blues music of the 1940s. Their movies played to slightly over six hundred theaters, most of which were located throughout the South. By 1946 reported *Newsweek*, Louis Jordan had become the best guarantee to pack those houses:

> Last week, the Negro film industry reached a new high-water mark with the release of "Beware," an Astor Pictures production starring Louis Jordan, one of Decca's most lucrative recorders, Valerie Black, former leading lady of the stage hit "Anna Lucasta," and Milton Woods, the "colored Basil Rathbone." The picture cinches Jordan's reputation as a great melody maker, but catchy tunes aside, "Beware" adds up to 55 minutes of heavy-handed melodrama inexpertly directed.

The presence of Jordan, who has just made his third personal appearance at the Paramount Theater in New York, assures "Beware's" box-office success. The most successful Negro film to date was "Caldonia," another Astor production with Jordan and his Tympany Five. Whether Jordan will confine his talents to all-Negro movies or follow the golden trail to Hollywood remains to be seen. Sultry Lena Horne's rapid rise to riches was furthered by her performances in "Boogie-Woogie Dream," a musical produced by Jack Goldberg, sometimes tagged the "Abe Lincoln of Harlem."

Goldberg, who has put out twenty-five Negro films in as many years, owns Hollywood Pictures Corp., an Astor rival in the Negro feature world. Both Astor and Hollywood studios are in New York. So are the studios of Quigley and Leonard and Toddy Pictures. Jack's brother Bert operates Harlemwood Pictures in Dallas.

The sixth of the largest Negro film producers is All American News of Chicago, which since 1942 has ground out more than 185 newsreels stressing Negro activities. Its 24-hour coverage now compares with that of Pathé, Movietone, and Paramount. Its latest venture is the "Negro Achievement Series"—documentaries combining news shots and reenactments in the style of "The March of Time."[1]

Many of the independent rhythm and blues record companies were formed after the Kansas City happening, World War II, and the initial spread of rhythm and blues music. Jubilee Records, which recorded the Orioles, was not founded until 1948; Atlantic, 1948; Herald/Ember, which recorded the Nutmegs and Joe Morris with Faye Adams, 1952; Chess, 1947; Vee Jay, 1953; Imperial, which recorded Fats Domino, 1947; Peacock, which eventually bought Duke, 1949; Dot, 1951; and Excello in Nashville, 1953. Not to be overlooked are those companies founded during or just after World War II: Apollo, 1942; Savoy, 1942; King, 1945; Aladdin, 1945; Modern, 1945; and several other small independent companies of earlier formation, such as Swing Time.

Charlie Gillett points out that there was definitely a period when few large companies recorded music aimed at the black communities:

By the end of the thirties, the major companies had a solid hold on the complete market for records, but during the war they yielded to the specialist "race" and "hillbilly" markets when forced to make economy cuts by the government ruling that customers must trade in an old record every time they bought a new one (so that the material could be melted down and used again). By the time the war ended and the majors could turn their attention back to the small markets, the independents had established a firm hold on both "race" and "hillbilly."[2]

It therefore seems highly probable that movies were instrumental in spreading the popularity of rhythm and blues. During the recording lull the most popular recording personality was Louis Jordan, and the music he played was rhythmic blues. Few people had television sets in 1946, and full-time radio programing for black people was not begun until 1948. In addition to records, motion pictures had a heavy impact upon the early spread of rhythm and blues music. The music existed in motion pictures as a primary source of entertainment for African-Americans, but certainly for any theater that wished to rent the films.

As late as 1954, before the release of the movie *Blackboard Jungle,* Jack Goldberg was still producing musicals for motion pictures. Unlike the dramas Astor produced with Louis Jordan, Studio Films, reported *Billboard,* produced a series of variety films which captured the top rhythm and blues and jazz performers of the day.

> Studio Films is now marketing a new series of three half hour musical shows which are being emceed by Willie Bryant, the self-styled "Mayor of Harlem." The variety show features some of the top Negro entertainers doing their singing and dancing specialties. Among the variety talent are Duke Ellington, Lionel Hampton, Count Basie, Sarah Vaughan, Ruth Brown, Amos Millium, the Orioles, Coles, and Atkins, and many other such top Negro artists. A great deal of interest has already been manifested in the series.[3]

When rhythm and blues began to explode on a national basis in 1955, Studio Films released two pictures with the expressed purpose of assisting the growing interest in the music. The releases coincided perfectly with the bomb that radio station WINS dropped on New York City in the person of Alan Freed.

> Rock and roll music and talent is getting a tremendous national build-up via the feature film, "Rock 'n' Roll Revue," produced by Studio Films, Inc., and already booked into more than 1,000 houses. Featuring top talent, such as Nat Cole, Lionel Hampton, Duke Ellington, the Clovers, Ruth Brown, Larry Darnell, Dinah Washington, Joe Turner, Willie Bryant, the Delta Rhythm Boys and Martha Davis, the film opens in New York October 24 in approximately 70 theaters. These include 28 RKO houses, 10 Skouras houses, eight Brandt theaters, three houses of the J & J Circuit and three of the Randforce chain. The film was released in April. . . .
>
> Studio Films is already booking another similar film, even more heavily flavored with rhythm and blues talent than the "Rock 'n' Roll Revue." This is called the "Rhythm and Blues Revue" and includes Count Basie, Joe Turner, Sarah Vaughan, Faye Adams, Lionel Hampton, Amos Milburn, Nat

Cole, Ruth Brown, the Larks, the Delta Rhythm Boys, Martha Davis, Paul
(Hucklebuck) Williams, Willie Bryant and others.[4]

The impact of motion pictures can also be traced back to the
present boom of country and western music. Originally captured and
further popularized in western movies by Gene Autry and Roy
Rogers, and other country western singers in the thirties, the music
in the early fifties was overshadowed by rhythm and blues. In the
mid-fifties country and western forces organized and attempted a
comeback through the screen, according to a story appearing in
Billboard in 1955 entitled "Country and Western Renaissance Due
Via Screen Push."

> Country and western music may be due for a renaissance judging by the
> bigtime Hollywood country and western musicals in the works for this year.
> MGM's long delayed film bio on the late Hank Williams' life is finally
> underway, with Jeff Richards reportedly tagged for the lead, while Paramount
> is looking for properties suitable, to showcase Elvis Presley, who was signed
> by the studio a couple of months ago.[5]

Similarly, though there was widespread interest in rhythm and
blues, white performers of the music did not become powerfully
popular among members of the larger society until they were captured in film aimed primarily at white audiences.

"Blackboard Jungle" and "Rock Around the Clock"

In 1950 Jerry Wexler wrote an article for *Saturday Review* de-
scribing five areas of musical expressions and categories comprising
the world of vocal rhythm and blues.

> Vocal blues are subdivided into the saccharine blues ballad (Charles Brown,
> The Orioles); the insinuating double-entendre blues (Little Esther, Amos
> Milburn); the shout blues (Wynonie Harris, Roy Brown); the primitive South-
> ern blues (John Lee Hooker, Smokey Hogg); the torch blues (Dinah Washing-
> ton, Ruth Brown), and still other subtypes.[6]

The shout category is a perfect description of Bill Haley who, as
Carl Belz said in his work *The Story of Rock,* tended to shout his
lyrics rather than to vocalize them cleanly. This category is also

descriptive of Joe Turner, affectionately called "the boss of the blues."

Turner, born in Kansas City, Missouri, May 18, 1911, was the first important blues band vocalist associated with swing bands of the Southwest territories. A bartender in various speakeasies in his hometown, Turner got into the habit of singing with the musicians who played in the spots where he worked, and became well known as a result of his association with one of them, pianist Pete Johnson, with whom he appeared at the famous 1938 Carnegie Hall "Spirituals to Swing" concert. After a period of several years away from the limelight, Turner reasserted his mastery of the urban blues approach with a strong series of recordings in the early 1950s, scoring a great success with his 1954 hit "Shake, Rattle and Roll."[7]

Bill Haley, originally from Detroit, led a country and western group which recorded "Shake, Rattle, and Roll" for the pop market. Initially known as the Saddlemen, they changed their name to Bill Haley and the Comets when they began performing rhythm and blues material around 1953. Like the wailing bands of blacks such as Big Jay McNeely, Haley's band employed movement and body action. They imitated to the extent of playing the saxophone while lying on the stage. More important, however, Haley and the Comets were successful with their imitations. Their 1954 recording of Turner's "Shake, Rattle, and Roll" sold in the millions. It is not surprising that publishers were sometimes deeply involved in covers.

After introducing a song in the rhythm and blues market, some publishers attempted to capitalize on covers by feeding a hot song to a pop artist or company in order to get more money from the larger white market. Not every cover or rhythm and blues song released with expectations of being a hit recording materialized. One such rhythm and blues song was "Rock Around the Clock" recorded by Sonny Dae in 1954, and covered by Bill Haley and his Comets. Haley's recording did not become very popular, but when Loew's filmed the motion picture *Blackboard Jungle,* Haley's cover was selected as the sound-track song. The movie, which made a star out of Sidney Poitier and starred Ann Francis, Glenn Ford, and Vic Morrow, also made a hit out of the song "Rock Around the Clock" and a legend out of Haley.

Some critics claimed that the movie did not paint a true picture of large urban schools. Many said that the movie's rhythm and blues theme song "Rock Around the Clock" presented to many people a new kind of music, as Freed called it, "rock and roll," which was associated with violence and juvenile delinquency.

In May 1955 *Ebony,* documenting the rise to fame of Sidney Poitier, probably best described the film.

> To the uninitiated, *Blackboard Jungle* depicts a school that is almost a house of horrors. A teacher is beaten up and left unconscious in an alley, his pregnant wife receives notes and phone calls hinting that he is running around with another woman, a pupil attempts to rape a young female teacher and another attacks Glenn Ford with a knife.
>
> Actually, producer Pandro S. Berman and Director Richard Brooks (he also directed *Take the High Ground* and *The Last Time I Saw Paris)* made an intensive study of juvenile delinquency in various big cities in preparation for making the movie. The events in *Blackboard Jungle* are similar to many that happen in "problem" high schools.
>
> Sidney Poitier has one of the most sympathetic roles in the movie. It is Poitier who finally helps the teacher win out in his attempt to reform his delinquent pubils.[8]

The film, also marketed early in 1955, coincided perfectly with the emerging interest in rhythm and blues and with the acquisition by New York City radio station WINS of Alan Freed from Cleveland, who instantly began calling rhythm and blues "rock and roll." Via New York's vogue setting power and Freed's instant popularity, the false name was the description under which critics chose to classify "Rock Around the Clock," which eventually sold a million copies in America, and spread abroad where it sold over 300,000 copies under the name of rock and roll. Whereas radio had given rhythm and blues national exposure, motion pictures became responsible for the international impact of the African-American music traveling under the name of rock and roll.

Blackboard Jungle also had more of a national or unified impact on America than did radio. Haley's cover of "Rock Around the Clock" was made a giant of a record via the film. By drawing attention to the music through the film production, rhythm and blues captured, for the first time, the number one spot on the pop charts in America as well as in England. The motion picture medium, tied the music together on a national scale. Radio failed to accomplish this because stations playing rhythm and blues served only regional areas. Alan Freed's "Rock and Roll Party" on the CBS radio network was aired after the release of *Blackboard Jungle,* and Willie Bryant's ABC radio network program was aired in May 1955. Both were half-hour shows.

The exposure of "Rock Around the Clock" in *Blackboard Jungle* caused uncontrollable emotions in some theaters, as witnessed by the disturbance at Princeton University in the late spring of 1955. These emotional outbursts only foreshadowed the response this African-American music would stimulate almost worldwide. Keeping in mind that these events were occurring in 1955, it becomes comprehensible that most young white Americans had little experience in African-American musical culture.

The rhythm and blues musicals of the great Louis Jordan which had been filmed during the forties were comedies such as *Caldonia* and *Beware,* and they never reached most whites even though Jordan is credited with breaking racial barriers when he played the West Coast in the late forties and early fifties. Segregation prevented general distribution of his films, and they played mostly to neighborhood theaters in the small African-American market. But it must be pointed out that the general American public in 1955 regarded Negro identity with about the same attitude as busing today. Therefore, only a white group such as Haley's could have reached the masses of young whites because of race identity, despite the fact that the music was still rhythm and blues. In a *Playboy* interview Ray Charles responded to a similar observation on identity:

White kids will never feel about Muddy Waters or B. B. King the way they feel about the Rolling Stones or Blood, Sweat and Tears. They've got to have entertainers from their own race to idolize, it seems. Negroes have been singing rhythm and blues, or soul music, as it's called today, since before I was born. But white mothers weren't going to let their daughters swoon over those black cats, so they never got widely known. Then along came Elvis Presley, and the white kids had a hero. All that talk about rock 'n' roll began then, but Black musicians started to get a little play, too. When the English boys came on the scene, they admitted where they got their inspiration and that caused even more interest in the real blues. I'm glad to see these youngsters doing our music. It enhances the guys who originated it, the same as one of those symphony orchestras enhances Beethoven.[9]

Without question, however, Bill Haley and the Comets were the most popular white performers of rhythm and blues in 1954 and early 1955. Haley stated in *Downbeat,* 1956, that his group had six hits prior to their "Rock Around the Clock" sound track. That song was strictly rhythm and blues, and the performers were white and sounded white. When young whites began embracing the sound track, they were in a sense accepting another culture's music and rejecting their parents' baritone idols. As Charlie Gillett wrote in his book *The Sound of the City:*

> By late 1955, Tony Bennett, and Perry Como were as obsolete as Bunny Berigan and Will Bradley, so far as the self-consciously youthful adolescents were concerned. The film version of *Blackboard Jungle* was a large success and much-discussed movie. What the presence in it of the music of Bill Haley, rather than of Tony Bennett and Perry Como, helped to establish in the minds of both adolescents and adults was the connection between rock and roll and teen-age rebellion.[10]

Alan Freed also had no illusions about the symbolism rhythm and blues represented to young whites. In a story he personally wrote for *Downbeat* in September 1955, Freed said: "But I think the reason that rock and roll is popular, with kids is that it represents a safe form of rebellion against authority."[11] Whereas "Shake, Rattle, and Roll" was a novelty, restless youth associated with "Rock Around the Clock" became an outright rebellion in the eyes of many white parents.

Partly because of society's ostracism of black American accomplishments and partly because of the identity factor mentioned by Ray Charles, young whites perceived the music in the film by Haley as something new. From the white perspective, Haley emerged from *Blackboard Jungle* as king of a new type of music, which from the black perspective was not valid. Even though blacks bought the well-produced record, Haley was not the best rhythm and blues performer. Haley could not surpass other rhythm and blues artists such as Joe Turner, Little Richard, the Midnighters, the Clovers, Bo Diddley, Fats Domino, the Drifters, Etta James, or B. B. King; but his side of the world happened to be larger. Hollywood ignored a ten-year or more legacy of rhythm and blues artists and circumvented all of the accomplishments and talent that blacks had to offer.

The Sonny Dae cover, however, became so popular via *Blackboard Jungle,* Sam Katzman contracted Haley to star in a rhythm and blues musical released by Columbia Pictures. The picture which billed Bill Haley and his Comets as the main attraction recognized other rhythm and blues performers; Freddy and the Bellhops and the now famous Platters as well. *Rock Around the Clock* not only brought money into the pockets of moviemakers, it opened wide the modern rhythm box of America's African descendents and unleashed a beat upon European-oriented culture which rocked its unemotional foundation.

Eighty percent of the movie was devoted to music: "See You Later, Alligator" and the "Great Pretender" by Haley and the Platters respectively were big hits. Altogether the movie had seventeen songs which left the audience breathless. What time was left to the story line attempted to show how a white band worked its way to top popularity.

Rhythm and Blues Films

The motion picture box office in the mid-fifties, like radio in the late forties and very early fifties, was hit hard by television. In late December 1956 Hollywood was claiming that *Rock Around the Clock* had grossed eight times its negative cost in the world market. As reported by *Variety,* rhythm and blues musicals became the brief savior of a Hollywood box office slump.

> In recent months exhibitors have clamored for film fare that would appeal to teen-age audiences whom they regard as their best customers. They called for pictures with built in teen appeal; that is based on subjects that arouse the interest of youngsters. In this category rock 'n' roll figures prominently.
>
> The teen films, many of them obvious "quickies" and "cheapies" made to take advantage of the market demand, succeed in fulfilling a theaterman's prime purpose—bringing customers to the box office.[12]

Sam Katzman had his finger resting comfortably on the world money pulse. Authorities employed to keep the peace did not understand the emotions young people were exhibiting in response to African rhythmic beats via the screen. Many theaters showing *Rock Around the Clock* experienced riots and many people in positions of power and authority "knocked the rock." But Katzman was apparently well aware of the old adage, "there's nothing more popular than being banned in Boston."

> In Boston, Roman Catholic leaders urged that the offensive music be boycotted. In Hartford, city officials considered revoking the State Theater's license after several audiences got too rowdy during a musical stage show. In Washington the police chief recommended banning such shows from the National Guard Armory after brawls in which several people were injured. In Min-

neapolis a theater manager withdrew a film featuring the music after a gang
of youngsters left the theater, snake-danced around town and smashed win-
dows. In Birmingham champions of white supremacy declared it as a part of
Negro plot against whites. At a wild concert in Atlanta's baseball park one
night, fists and beer bottles were thrown, four youngsters were arrested.[13]

By late 1956 *Rock Around the Clock* had reached England. Response by audiences there put authorities into frenzies. Whereas
radio had exposed rhythm and blues in the United States, motion
pictures spread the music upon the international scene, and England's teen-agers loved it no less than Americans.

Despite continued outbreaks of rowdyism, arrests and at times theater prop-
erty damage, the Rank Organization will continue to play Columbia's "Rock
Around the Clock" in its circuits.
   During the previous two weeks when the film was going the rounds in
northwest and northeast London, theater managers on several occasions had
to call police. Frequently "Feddy Boys" left their seats to rock and roll in the
aisles.[14]

In smaller communities of England authorities felt less comfort-
able about showing the film. Reports from Manchester, England,
indicated that *Rock Around the Clock* received the same fashionable
welcome as it had in Boston.

"Rock Around the Clock" has now been banned in Wegan, South Shields,
Bootie, Gateshead, Brighton, and Birmingham.
   An Alderman in Gateshead: "We think it's undesirable that the film should
be shown here, and that the public should have to put up with this sort of
hooliganism."[15]

Sam Katzman's second film with Haley had an added attraction,
Alan Freed. Freed was popular in New York, and by 1956 his name
was a nationwide household word. Katzman's aim was to bring the
most popular personalities of rhythm and blues together in film. The
movie which was eventually called *Don't Knock the Rock* and also
featured Little Richard and the Treniers had a brilliant opportunity
to place rock and roll in the proper perspective, but failed. The
movie, according to *Variety,* was to have been originally entitled
Rhythm and Blues.

Haley wound up his second film for Sam Katzman over the weekend and
trekked out for more P.A.'s which will help exploit the film which Katzman

is rushing into release within the next six weeks. Feature originally was called "Rhythm and Blues" but final title may be "Don't Knock the Rock" from a tune of that title by Robert E. Keat and Fred Karger which is prominently featured in the film.[16]

Don't Knock the Rock was distributed with a youth gang war film called *Rumble on the Docks.* Even though *Don't Knock the Rock* attempted to disprove the adverse publicity rhythm and blues was receiving, *Rumble on the Docks* only seemed to marry violence and rebellion to the music.

By this time, however, late 1956, almost a dozen rhythm and blues films were being polished for release, all of which were aimed directly at the teen-age market:

> Following up its successful "Rock Around the Clock" which is expected to gross eight times its negative cost in the world market, Columbia now has "Don't Knock the Rock" and "Cha-Cha-Boom." At 20th "Love Me Tender" is being followed with a semi-rock 'n' roller "The Girl Can't Help It."
>
> Universal has "Rock Pretty Baby" which it's selling as a June romance, and United Artists has Abbott and Costello in "Dance with Me Henry" this month. Distributors Corp. of America is releasing "Rock, Rock, Rock," and American International has delivered "Shake, Rattle, and Roll" and is planning to put out a follow-up.
>
> Companies feel that their rock 'n' roll releases serve the very useful purposes of luring the juve audience sector *back* to the B.O.[17]

The broad exposure of rhythm and blues music through film lifted the music to heights never dreamed possible by its early performers. Possibly *Blackboard Jungle* brought an unexpected success to "Rock Around the Clock." However, when Haley and the Platters sang "See You Later Alligator" and "The Great Pretender" in the movie *Rock Around the Clock,* it was no stroke of luck that the records topped popularity charts. Cinema has a long history of significant impact and influence upon our society, and it did not take long to discover that such powers also applied to the new musical explosion.

Motion picture appearance and exposure of artist and song had a high correlation with chart appearance. "Be Bop A Lula" by Gene Vincent, "Blue Monday" by Fats Domino, and "You'll Never Know" by the Platters all appeared in the movie *The Girl Can't Help It,* and all of the recordings were hits. The film title song was released by Specialty's Little Richard, and it remains a classic. Other motion picture songs had similar successes. In *Rock, Rock, Rock,* Chuck

Berry, La Vern Barker, the Moonglows, the Teenagers, and the Flamingos all managed hits. In some cases, however, the songs preceded the film appearance.

Though most of the movies were filmed in black and white and cheaply produced (*The Girl Can't Help It* was an exception), their influence was far reaching. Most youngsters saw their idols via the film medium, and they studied them well. Wholeheartedly they absorbed the dance routines, "hip" talk, and imitated the singers. From motion pictures the casual dress of rock stars began to emerge. Guitar bands held together by a single drummer became popular. Many of the films had integrated casts, black and white performers, but none of the movies ever credited black Americans for having created the rock music. And young white Americans began cornering a market as their own.

REFERENCES

1. *Newsweek,* Vol. 28 (July 8, 1946), p. 85.

2. Charlie Gillett, *The Sound of the City* (New York: Outerbridge and Dienstfrey, 1970), pp. 7–8.

3. *Billboard,* Vol. 66 (September 4, 1954), p. 6.

4. "Rock and Roll Revue," *Billboard,* Vol. 67 (October 8, 1955), p. 17.

5. "Rock and Roll Country Talent," *Billboard,* Vol. 68 (May 12, 1956), p. 12.

6. Jerry Wexler, "Rhythm and Blues in 1950," *Saturday Review,* Vol. 38 (June 24, 1950), p. 49.

7. Pete Welding, *Urban Blues,* Vol. 1, Imperial LM 94002.

8. "Blackboard Jungle," *Ebony,* Vol. 5 (May 1955) p. 87.

9. *Playboy Magazine,* Vol. 17 (March 1970), p. 69.

10. Gillett, *op. cit.,* p. 20.

11. Freed, *op. cit.,* p. 44.

12. *Variety,* Vol. 205 (December 19, 1956), p. 1.

13. *Time,* Vol. 67 (June 18, 1956), p. 54.

14. *Variety,* Vol. 204 (September 12, 1956), p. 2.

15. "Rock Around the Clock," *Variety,* Vol. 204 (September 19, 1956), p. 2.

16. "Rock and Roll is Getting Bigger All the Time," *Variety,* Vol. 204 (September 26, 1956), p. 7.

17. *Variety*, Vol. 205 (December 5, 1956), p. 5.

CHAPTER 4.

Television

Post World War II Television

AFTER WORLD WAR II THE TELEVISION INDUSTRY SOUGHT TO encourage advertisers to use the new medium. Millions of dollars had been poured into television, and very small financial return had yet been realized. There were some minor debates as to whether commercial television programing was developed extensively enough for the public to accept. But television had survived World War II, and in the final analysis the video medium took its place within the American society.

In 1948 there were only seventeen TV stations on the air, another fifty-five under construction, and sixty-six license applications pending. The Federal Communications Commission had only recently approved A.T.&T.'s $76,000,000 expansion program aimed at extending coaxial cable circuits south to Charlotte and as far west as Chicago and St. Louis. The National Broadcasting Company felt assured enough to predict a cross-country television network by 1950. Much of the programing during this time was locally originated, and in numerous instances African-Americans made valuable contributions. For those Americans who had sets, mostly whites, the televising of African-American artists brought into view a whole new world of comedy, dance, and music.

African-Americans and Early Television

The most popular black personality on the West Coast was Hadda Brooks, who had gained success nationally on the Modern record label. Hadda began recording for Modern in 1945 and had tremendous success with songs such as "Swing the Boogie," "Riding the Boogie," and "Rocking the Boogie." Her recording of "That's My Desire" sold over a million records. Hadda was graduated from the University of Southern California with a degree in music, and her husky voice which exuded sex needed only brief video exposure to propel the Hadda Brooks Show into the hearts of West Coast viewers. The Hadda Brooks Show, however, was not aimed primarily at a black audience. *Ebony* in April 1951 covered the success of Hadda's video landmark:

> Television fans on the West Coast, stuck with a steady video fare of second-rate ex-vaudeville entertainers and old movies until a coaxial cable is completed back to the East (perhaps not before 1953), are finding a refreshing treat on their sets at least once a week in a live telecast featuring sultry pianist-vocalist Hadda Brooks, longtime recording and night club favorite. First aired as a Sunday night feature from Los Angeles station KLAC-TV, the songs and patter of the charming night club star are now sponsored by Kaiser-Frazer on a half-hour Tuesday night program on San Francisco's KGO-TV.
>
> Called simply *The Hadda Brooks Show,* the telecast plays up the kind of nostalgic melodies and folksy chatter that clicks with audiences everywhere, no matter what the medium. Most radio columnists list the show among the best TV bets, and surveys show that it draws a big audience of video viewers.
>
> Format used by Hadda on TV is simple. She accompanies herself on piano, projecting her tunes softly and melodiously at a relaxed pitch. Her vocal offerings are mostly old tunes like "I Hadn't Anyone 'Til You," "Don't Take Your Love from Me," and "You Won't Let Me Go," which she introduces in low, almost whispered tones. She writes the script and selects all the songs for her show.[1]

The first all-black television program is said to have taken place in Chicago, which by 1949 was a kingpin city for rhythm and blues. Under today's classification the show's description would place it in the jazz vein. In 1949, descriptions of various types of secular black music were relatively unimportant. Black people just did their thing. The Chicago show was aimed directly toward blacks, and its audience was identified as such.

> WENR-TV will telecast the first all-Negro television show April 1, titled "Happy Pappy." Weekly program will bring top names of Sarah Vaughan and Ella Fitzgerald, but also maintain search for new talent. Entire cast and studio audience will be all-Negro.
>
> Vagabonds will back musically, while Ray Grant will emcee.[2]

The Nat Cole Trio, having scored big hit recordings of "Straighten Up and Fly Right" and "Route 66" became very popular in the late forties and influenced many struggling young performers. The great Ray Charles came under Cole's influence and with his own trio landed a television show in 1953.

> He toured for a year with Lowell Fulson's blues band and later formed a combo to back vocalist Ruth Brown. Then he did an unnoticed single at Harlem's Apollo Theater. Back in Seattle, things began to pick up when the Maxim Trio, a group he put together in 1953, became the first Black act to get its own sponsored television show in the Pacific Northwest.[3]

The real rhythm and blues exposure in local television was in the South. Just how pervasive the televising was cannot be documented at this writing, but Ruth Cage in her famous *Downbeat* series on rhythm and blues indicated Atlanta, Georgia, was one southern city where the music was aired on TV.

> Chuck's [Willis] first national success came in 1952 when he wrote and recorded "My Story." In Atlanta there was a year of TV and lots more jobs in clubs there. Deejay Zenis Spears, in the home town, was a Willis fan and presented him often on his "Blues Caravans."[4]

Compared to the vastness of today's television programing, early shows with blacks may seem in retrospect minimal and insignificant. However, the local employment of blacks on television in the late forties and early fifties seems to have been influenced by a national guideline or established practice.

Whether the national television industry was responding from the heart or from pressure groups remains in question. The NAACP has a long history of network vigilance and perseverance for fair exposure for African-Americans. In 1953 the National Broadcasting Company delivered a progress report to the black community assuring its citizens that equality was being achieved.

> NBC booked a total of 218 Negro acts and individual performers in the past two years, with the 1952 figures representing a 200% increase over 1951, veepee Edward D. Madden said in a "progress report to the Negro community."
>
> Madden said that counting repeat performances there was a total of 450 performances by Negro Artists, not including the Billy Williams Quartet, Dorothy Dandridge, or Lillian Randolph, each of whom has had regular niches. Including musicians and members of performing groups, there was an

estimated 1,540 performances in radio and 913 in TV by Negroes. NBC, V.P. said.[5]

By 1953 the broad range of African-American entertainment in the new medium had been well established, if not through the efforts of the National Broadcasting Company then through those of CBS. In 1948 the Columbia Broadcasting System hired a former vaudeville producer and syndicated journalist (who had also been cited by the United States government for war work in hospitals and camps) to headline an hour-long variety show on Sunday evenings. The affable gentleman who was as well-received in uptown New York City with blacks as with the white power structure moved in a maze of respected circles and contacts. The Ed Sullivan Show was appropriately christened "The Toast of the Town."

By October of the same year, 1948, the "Toast of the Town" topped television ratings which were conducted in New York City and Philadelphia. *Broadcasting* printed The Pulse Inc. results: "Toast of the Town Tops TV Ratings." The top ten television network programs carried simultaneously by stations in New York and Philadelphia in September, as reported last week in a two-city survey by The Pulse Inc., were (figure given is average rating of highest quarter-hour):

Toast of the Town WCBS-TV, WCAU-TV Sunday	38.8
Texaco Star Theatre WNBT, WPTZ Tuesday	37.9
Boxing WCBS-TV, WCAU-TV Monday	31.1
Small Fry Club WABD, WFIL-TV Monday through Friday	25.2
Original Amateur Hour WABD, WFIL-TV Sunday	24.8
Winner Take All WCBS-TV, WCAU-TV Wednesday	20.7
We, the People WCBS-TV, WCAU-TV Tuesday	18.5
Kraft TV Theatre WNBT, WPTZ Wednesday	17.6
Gay Nineties Revue WABD-TV, WFIL-TV Wednesday	15.9[6]

African-American contributions were an intricate and important part of Sullivan's success in the new video medium. In fact, enough blacks had found an outlet through Sullivan's show that *Ebony* magazine contracted the columnist to write a story for them which appeared in the May 1951 issue. In the story entitled "Can TV Crack America's Color Line," Sullivan reflected and praised the tremendous contributions blacks had made to early television. He used black performers in practically every one of his shows and openly admitted he could not have gotten along without W. C. Handy (Father of the Blues), Lena Horne, Ethel Waters, Bill Robinson, Peg-Leg Bates (the great one-legged dancer), Jackie Robinson, Billy Eckstine, or Pigmeat Markham. All of them added significantly to Sullivan's success, and he withheld no credit or praise.

I've never used a Negro act on *Toast of the Town,* which has failed to enjoy a tremendous success. The new medium is made to order for Negroes and it has been proven on my program by Illinois Jacquet, Ruby Hill, Sarah Vaughan, the Kingdom Choir, Roll and Tapp, Moke and Poke, the magnificant Deep River Boys, Golden Gate Quartet, Tables Davis, Cab Calloway, Ella Fitzgerald, Louis Jordan, Nat "King" Cole, Louis Armstrong, Hazel Scott, the Ink Spots, Son and Sonny, and Brother Jones. These acts, always great, became greater on television because everyone in the TV audience has a front-row seat.

The Negro performer never abuses the hospitality he finds in American homes. Invariably—and this has been commented upon by all the 70 people who work on our show—The Negro performer's material is clean. Some of the white performers, at dress rehearsals, utter lines that would cancel us off the air and are astonished when told such lines must be deleted. The white transgressor always makes the same statement: "They let me do it at the Roxy," or whatever theatres they've played recently. The Negro, perhaps because of the fact that he has forever been on trial, instinctively rejects the dubious line or gesture.

Recognizing the place of the Negro in television is not generosity. It is just common sense and good business. In fact, if there has been generosity, television has received it from the Negro. In the first place, you just can't have great programs unless you integrate the Negro performer into a show. In the second place, it has never been pointed out that the Negro performer has been a great friend to television. I personally know that, without his generous help, the early TV days would have been a nightmare.

Those were the early, lean days when there wasn't much money in TV for any of us.

"Look, Ed," said Peg-Leg Bates, "Why discuss money. I started in vaudeville with you—in your act. Let's talk friendship, not money."

So Peg-Leg came on the show and panicked them. The same with Billy Kenny and the Ink Spots.

"You've been for us. We're for you," they said. They came on those early shows, not once but three times. On one show, the Ink Spots agreed to serve as an opening act, although they are headliners.

"Turn us loose first," said Billy Kenny. "People will think you must have a powerful show if you're leading off with us."

Louis Jordan appeared in those slim days—because he'd been introduced to Broadway on a vaudeville show of mine.

Sarah Vaughan acted the same way—and if I ever tried to express my debt of personal appreciation to Joe Louis, I'd be writing all night long.

"I need help, Joe," I told him over the phone.

"Just tell me what time to be on hand, Ed," he said.

That was a few nights after the first Joe Walcott fight and Louis unhesitatingly came up on the stage, took off his sun glasses and exposed his shiner.

They didn't get much money—the Negro performers—very little, in fact, but when I needed help—when the squalling infant industry of television needed help, the Negro star was loyal and considerate. Many white performers were equally kind, but too many of them turned their heads the other way.[7]

It is inconceivable that through all of this exposure, rhythmic blues was not viewed throughout America. Somehow, sometime the grassroots culture had to come through. Cab Calloway was an exciting hoofer, the Jackie Wilson of his day; Illinois Jacquet could blow the reed off a saxophone; and the fetes of Louis Jordan have already been covered.

Sam Charters, mentioned in *The Country Blues* that T-Bone Walker, the top blues performer at that time, made appearances on the Ed Sullivan Show in the early fifties. The degree of rhythm and blues exposure remained minimal, however, and it is still a rarity for a heavy rhythm and blues artist to perform more than one song on most established television shows. Yet television's history is not without a significant thrust and impact upon the development of rhythm and blues popularity.

Billy Ward and the Arthur Godfrey Show

In the late forties, young multi-talented Billy Ward was working as an artist in an advertising agency operated by Rose Marks. She encouraged Ward to open an arranging and vocal coaching studio, which he did. He had studied at Juilliard and the Chicago Art Institute. Billy Ward organized some of his students into a singing group. The group was composed of Cliff Givens, Milton Merle,

James Van Loan, Jackie Wilson, Clyde McPhatter, and Billy Ward. They called themselves the Dominos and hired Rose Marks as their manager. In October 1950 they appeared on the Arthur Godfrey Talent Scout Show and came away as winners.

Later that year the Dominos became the most popular and successful group in rhythm and blues history with the recording of "Sixty Minute Man." Another rocker recording entitled "Have Mercy, Mercy, Baby" solidified their success, and Ward groomed his singers to perform a wide range of material while still maintaining the African work-song structure and influence. It was the success of the Dominos, along with that of the Orioles, which broke rhythm and blues from its ostracized musical bars and put it on the pop charts, thus triggering the rhythm and blues explosion. Television helped to make the Dominos nationally important and served as an important springboard to perhaps the greatest rhythm and blues vocal group of all time.

Television continued to program blacks but provided very little exposure for rhythm and blues. Lena Horne and the Billy Williams Quartet played the Sid Caesar-Imogene Coca Show. Other blacks such as the Lionel Hampton Quartet were guests on various variety shows such as "Shower of Stars." At times there were sparkling instances where television pointed vividly toward the humanitarian tool it seeks to achieve. The Mariners, an integrated quartet composed of two blacks and two whites, were regulars on the Arthur Godfrey Television Show. Although their music was barber shop-middle of the road, the governor of Georgia could not tolerate them.

In 1952 Godfrey was asked to comment on Georgia Governor Herman Talmadge's denunciation of his show because it included a mixed singing quartet. Coldly angry, Godfrey said, "Would you kindly tell Governor Talmadge for me that if these four young fellows could fight together through a war in behalf of our United States where bullets didn't bother with segregation, that I'm afraid I can't bother with it either."[8]

Network TV
and African-American Programing

Rhythm and blues music represented, as it still does, a highly detectable portion of Afro-American culture. And despite the tremendous recording success of the Dominos, the Orioles, the Clovers, the Drifters, Ruth Brown, or Ray Charles, the video industry apparently did not take rhythmic blues seriously until 1956. In retrospect, Ed Sullivan in the midst of extreme criticism of rock and roll music made an historic and formidable move. In November 1955 he presented an hour-long rhythm and blues "Toast of the Town Show."

> TV, as well as radio, has played an increasing part in bringing rock and roll and rhythm and blues talent into the home. Dr. Jive, eminent rhythm and blues deejay, was booked on the Ed Sullivan TV show November 20 [1955]. Dr. Jive lined up the talent and emceed the show, which featured La Vern Baker, Bo Diddley, the Five Keys and Willis Jackson's work.
>
> Sullivan is putting together another "Toast of the Town" show, scheduled for the summer featuring rhythm and blues, jazz and bop talent.[9]

Studio Films, Inc., however, was away ahead of Sullivan. The degree of success which the firm had in booking is unknown, but in August 1954 *Downbeat* discovered twenty-six artists were being filmed for television by the New York firm.

> Studio Films, Inc., is the latest operation to recognize the cash potential of rhythm and blues. The television outfit is filming twenty-six TV shorts with a top artist from the field headlining each one. The picture makers aren't tampering with the basic rhythm and blues beat, but they are putting some fancy production into the films with veteran performer-producer Leonard Reed acting as director.
>
> Harlem's "mayor," Willie Bryant, will emcee all of the series. Most of the names were drawn from the Shaw Artists roster—Faye Adams and Ruth Brown were among the first to be lensed—with other agencies contributing such stars as Roy Hamilton.[10]

By spring of 1956 rhythm and blues was too popular nationwide for the rest of television to ignore. The potential of greenbacks finally convinced the networks to cease satirizing the music and to recognize its powerful audience possibility when presented as straight entertainment. Sullivan had made his point. After all, no one in television could top his current popularity: Best TV MC, 1953; Best TV Variety Program, 1954–55; Best TV Network Program, 1954–55, in Fame-MP Daily Poll; Best TV Network Program, 1954. When Sullivan recognized rhythm and blues in such an embraceable manner, the rest of television could no longer deny it.

The programing wheels of mass communication's most powerful medium commenced to turn. But it was America 1956; and when the wheels stopped, African-Americans were denied admittance across the color line. The article Sullivan had written for *Ebony* five years earlier had been answered. No! Television would not break America's color line.

Initial activity in the early spring of 1956 had indicated a tremendous interest in programing rhythm and blues. Alan Freed was negotiating to present a half-hour rock and roll television bill on Jackie Gleason's "Stage Show." An hour-long rhythm and blues show was being mulled over for Al (Jazzbo) Collins to emcee on Friday nights. At the same time NBC was preparing a Saturday afternoon show for teen-agers to be aired from 5:00 to 6:00 P.M. If Freed clicked, a chance as permanent emcee on "Stage Show" awaited him next season. In view of these considerations, somehow, network rhythm and blues shows lost out.

The final decisions on considerations to program network rhythm and blues shows left the music without a video showcase. It is inconceivable that the question of race never entered the picture. That element had long influenced rhythm and blues music. The Alabama white citizens council led the fight in 1956. Also, the music licensing firms, ASCAP and BMI, which television pays millions annually for programing thousands of songs, were at odds with each other because of the popularity increase of rhythm and blues.

Some people in the music business strongly believed that much of the controversy over rhythm and blues music during the mid-fifties was actually manufactured by ASCAP, the American Society of Composers, Authors, and Publishers. In 1956 Alan Freed told *Look* that ASCAP would not even license rhythm and blues at one time:

> The old-timers who formerly controlled the music publishing business wouldn't even license rhythm and blues material until about a year ago [1955]. By that time, a new group of writers and publishers had gotten the inside track on rock and roll and now the newcomers are making the money.[11]

If rhythm and blues was regularly programed on television, undoubtedly ASCAP was going to lose some ground to Broadcast Music Inc. (BMI). The power of television to make a song was staggering. "The Ballad of Davy Crockett" from Walt Disney's ABC-TV series became the all great recording; and "Let Me Go Lover," exposed by television in early 1955, exploded into prominence after it had been declared a bomb or flop. What then would television do to further popularize a new type music which was already adopted by most young Americans? Rhythm and blues had already gained strong programing in radio, chart appearance, and this was hurting ASCAP and helping BMI.

The desire by some people to keep rhythm and blues from a power position was basically twofold in nature. 'We've suggested," wrote Ruth Cage, in *Downbeat,*

> . . . that the basis for the big battle had something to do with the question of cash; Mr. Freed has suggested it has something to do with a social problem. Chances are that there is something of each of these factors in the whole business.[12]

Freed had the racism angle computed right from the start:

> To me, this campaign against Rock and Roll smells of discrimination of the worst kind against the great and accomplished Negro songwriters, musicians, and singers who are responsible for this outstanding contribution to American music.[13]

Robert Blair Kaiser cut open the real heart of the issue fifteen years later and exposed the truth in retrospect:

> It was Elvis who first dared give the people a music that hit them where they lived, deep in their emotions, yes, even below their belts. Oh, other singers had been doing this for generations, but they were black. They didn't count, at least where records were sold, because little white girls in middle America had a hard time getting any kind of fantasy going with a black man. It was easy, though, with Elivs.[14]

Another factor which seems to bear significantly on the denial of a national rhythm and blues show was the absence of an African-American program from the networks. Almost any show could have spotlighted rhythm and blues performers just as the Amos and Andy radio series had worked in the gospel groups such as the Jubilaires and Delta Rhythm Boys. This could have been a beginning.

When Amos and Andy moved to television in 1952 with an all-black cast rather than Freeman Gosden and Charles Correll, who were both white, an old friend awaited them. Some people believed the show hurt more than helped the black people. A successful campaign was waged to remove the show from network programming and in the process, explained the 1952 *Negro Year Book,* television was given an excuse not to program black shows.

> The National Association for the Advancement of Colored People, however, protested the sterotyping alleged to be present in this show, causing confusion

in the TV studios. Should they disregard the rising storm, strengthened by
the additional opposition of Phi Beta Sigma, one of the leading college frater-
nities?

These protests occurred at a time when it was rumored the studios were
about ready to go forward in the employment of Negro artists in a large way.
In this emergency, a Coordinating Council was organized in New York in
July 1951, by the Negro Actors Guild in response to public request.

Since the Guild is a welfare organization, the Council became a separate
entity. It aims at promoting better understanding in the selection of script
material for Negro parts, without caricatures and stereotypes, and at ac-
quainting producers and sponsors with the wealth of available Negro talent.
The Council will adopt a positive approach to the solution of differences,
looking to mutually beneficial results. It is interracial and includes representatives from the amusement world and the press as well as individuals and
representatives of outside organizations.[15]

Black oriented programing by the networks never fully materialized on television. As the years passed, the number of locally produced programs featuring blacks decreased as network programing,
without blacks, increased. Network television, which decided not to
recover from the action against stereotype programing of African-
Americans, found it easier to program very little or none at all. Guest
shots, of course, continued.

Rhythm and blues was affected because it was a music of the
masses; grassroots black America, not the middle-class decision
makers who may have preferred opera or European classics to
rhythm and blues music. Rhythm and blues was performed by the
slick heads and most of the artists performed on what Lou Rawls
calls "the "chittlin' circuit." The most vivid place this author brings
to mind is the "State Line," a little wooden dance shack which sat
in the middle of a cotton patch just outside of Blythville, Arkansas,
and very close to the Missouri state line. The sharecroppers in the
area as well as their poor urban counterparts supported the entire
spectrum of rhythm and blues for years with their nickels and dimes
from the soil and from the bottom of this country's economic scale.
Who involved in the television industry could represent their interests when in fact no avenue of African-American culture had a
network showcase?

Coinciding with television programing that omitted rhythm and
blues was the network appearance of Elvis Presley. His television
appearance eventually led to the separation of the musical terms
rhythm and blues and rock and roll, which until 1956 had been used
synonymously or interchangeably.

The Rise of Elvis Presley

In the fall of 1955 Presley played for the annual Country and Western Disc Jockey Association's fall convention in Nashville, Tennessee. Two talent scouts from RCA Victor, one of whom was the late Steve Shols, talked their company into purchasing Presley's recording contract from Sam Phillips' Sun Records of Memphis for $40,000. Though small by today's vast record market, that sum of money was astronomical for a contract involving an unknown in 1955. Shoals for awhile became the laughingstock of many people inside the record industry. Phillips agreed to the sale because he alledgedly did not think Elvis, a young white singing rhythm and blues, would last.

Recording companies by 1956 knew the importance of artist exposure via television and attempted to establish cooperation with the medium as a means of increasing record sales. This was especially true if megacompany ties existed, according to *Variety* in mid-1956.

> Diskeries are particularly keen on getting their personalities on the big video shows either via guest shots or regular series. Those labels with network affiliation to promote such appearances and closer liaison, especially between the RCA Victor and NBC web, is being established to keep it "in the family."[16]

In order to cover the huge investment it had made in purchasing Presley's contract RCA felt that video exposure was essential. Elvis who had once been denied an opportunity to compete on the Arthur Godfrey Talent Scouts when he was an independent, now had RCA behind him. When Presley visited New York, he also visited the Apollo Theater in Harlem. There many of the blues men were performing stage routines similar to T-Bone Walker, who had once been a dancer. Bo Diddley who was recording for Chess Records, influenced by Walker's routine, was very popular, and some of Presley's new image was identical to Bo Diddley's.

Elvis Presley, unlike Bill Haley, was not a "Johnny-come-lately" imitator of rhythm and blues. His love for African-American music was genuine, and on occasion he visited Rev. H. W. Brewster's church on East Trigg in Memphis. He also had some rhythm and blues idols such as Arthur "Big Boy" Crudup, Junior Parker, and Chuck Willis. Some of his first recordings for Sun Records were previously popularized by these men. And when Presley performed on the country and western circuit during his prefame days, he sang rhythm and blues songs such as "I Got a Woman," made famous by Ray Charles, and "Long Tall Sally," by Little Richard. However, this is not to say that he did not sing any country and western music.

That spring in 1956 RCA dropped its bombshell on television. Jackie Gleason was producing a big band television program called "Stage Show," which featured Jimmy and Tommy Dorsey. One Saturday Presley, making a guest appearance, wiggled across the television screen and mumbled rhythm and blues in a manner most television audiences had never seen before. The rhythm and blues style of body movement accompanying the song left adult white America breathless, but in a rage.

The lover's lament, "Heartbreak Hotel," which Presley sang on "Stage Show" was the hottest record in the nation and his coos— Joe Turner-styled mumbles—and cries thrust themselves into the hearts of young girls the country over. For the first time young white Americans had an idol of the new music all to themselves, a real live sex idol. Through his live appearances, Presley had been pleasing young audiences for nearly a year, but it was television that brought to most young white Americans their hero, their king of a music, known to them only as rock and roll.

With the coming of Elvis Presley, rhythm and blues—the music Alan Freed called rock and roll to spread its popularity among young whites—suddenly took on a new meaning. Under the popularity of Presley, made into a legend through six appearances on "Stage Show," rock and roll began to be identified as something different from rhythm and blues. And by the end of 1956 white America was claiming rock and roll as their own young musical culture:

> Rock and roll, which is now identified virtually as a distinct idiom, produced its own share of new chart artists.[17]

Elvis Presley did not cover other rhythm and blues artists. He recorded classic rhythm and blues material such as Hound Dog and several songs previously recorded and written by Arthur Crudup including My Baby Left Me. Basically his material was original and his success without "covering" established a trend for the new chart winners. As the late Buddy Holly once put it: "Without Elvis Presley, none of us could have made it."

The difference between the new chart winners of the so-called new idiom was arbitrary. Such artists as the Diamonds, the Crickets, the Four Aces, and Pat Boone were placed in rock and roll. Artists such as Ray Charles, the Drifters, and Ruth Brown were kept in the original idiom of rhythm and blues. The issue was, though unspoken, visibly one of white and black.

Almost twenty years later, a group of recording executives would call a conference in Los Angeles to determine what separated rhythm and blues (soul) from rock and roll (pop). H.B. Barnum, a well-known and respected arranger, analyzed the boundaries this way:

> I've got an overdub session to go to in a few minutes. I'm recording Don Ho. That will be classified a pop record. If I take the same background singers, charts and musicians and put them behind Lou Rawls, it will be called a rhythm and blues record.[18]

He was right. The impact of mass media had created a false dichotomy between rhythm and blues and rock and roll.

REFERENCES

1. "Hadda Brooks," *Ebony,* Vol. 6 (April 1951), p. 103.

2. *Variety,* Vol. 173 (March 9, 1949), p. 1.

3. *Playboy* Magazine, Vol. 17 (March 1970), p. 68.

4. "Rhythm and Blues," *Downbeat,* Vol. 21 (August 25, 1954), p. 21.

5. "NBC-No Color," *Variety,* Vol. 190 (March 18, 1953) p. 1.

6. "Toast of Town Tops TV Ratings," *Broadcasting,* Vol. 35 (October 18, 1948), p. 32.

7. Ed Sullivan, "Can TV Crack America's Color Line," *Ebony,* Vol. 6 (May 1951), p. 62.

8. *Ebony,* Vol. 9 (February 1954), p. 83.

9. Paul Ackerman, "All Are Getting Hip," *Billboard,* Vol. 68 (February 4, 1956), p. 1.

10. *Downbeat,* August 25, 1954.

11. *Look,* Vol. 20 (June 26, 1956), p. 48.

12. Cage, "Rhythm and Blues," *Downbeat,* Vol. 22 (April, 20, 1955), p. 41.

13. *Downbeat,* Vol. 22 (April 20, 1955), p. 41.

14. Robert Kaiser, "The Rediscovery of Elvis," *New York Times Magazine,* October 11, 1970, p. 47.

15. Jessie Guzman, ed. *The Negro Year Book* (New York: Wm. H. Wise and Company, 1952).

16. *Variety,* Vol. 203 (July 11, 1956), p. 41.

17. *Billboard,* Vol. 68 (January 26, 1957), p. 58.

18. *Billboard* (December 2, 1972), p. 65.

CHAPTER 5

Summary and Conclusions

IN EARLY 1960 HANK BALLARD AND THE MIDNIGHTERS—WHO had caused an uproar among broadcasting and music critics a half decade earlier with "Sexy Ways" and "Work With Me Annie"— rereleased a song called "The Twist," which Ballard had written and issued previously as a "B" side to an earlier rhythm and blues hit. "The Twist" described a dance which captivated teen-agers; and the song, recorded also by Chubby Checker, sold into the millions.

By the summer of 1961 the Twist was the vogue with eastern Yankee dancers. On the west side of New York City people were twisting every night in a saloon called the Peppermint Lounge to the music of Joey Dee and the Starlighters, which later became a nationally known group.

Whether the Twist spread by air or by word of mouth on subways is not known, but somehow the jet set got the news that the cats down in the alley were having more fun despite their lack of wealth. The jet set, by their acceptance of the Twist, not only broke a cultural barrier but signaled that rock music could no longer be degraded as mere unattractive noise. The Twist had suddenly made the music what was happening. And the derogatory remarks of nearly a decade before ceased to be voiced.

While white America was mesmerized by the Twist, rhythm and blues was undergoing still another significant experience. Ray Charles, whose excellence encompasses the complete spectrum of black music and beyond, released in 1961 an instrumental jazz arrangement of "One Mint Julep," a song written by Rudolph Toombs and initially recorded by the Clovers in 1952. The song stirred the soul of black America. Right in the middle of the song the band stopped long enough to hear Ray Charles moan, "just a little bit of soul now." Some people argued that Charles had said soda not soul, but from that time on the expression "soul," which had been used among black musicians for years, began to spread throughout black America.

When Ray Charles called for "just a little bit of soul" from his band, the musicians increased the beauty of their performance with greater expression and intensity. They responded with an emotional quality of excellence which could not be measured, only felt by those who shared the African experience. That musical response became a source of pride, which young black Americans began to associate with superior performance.

The language of the people was diffused to black radio announcers, who were in fact a part of the people. They began to speak of the "soul" certain performers were exhibiting in their music. "He's got soul," "She's got soul," or "The band has a lot of soul." By 1964 black-oriented stations were being referred to as "soul stations," and in turn rhythm and blues began to assume the identity of soul music.

In the meantime, in 1962 the Beatles initiated the English invasion, and they were followed by other British groups such as the Dave Clark Five, Gerry and the Pacemakers, the Animals, and the Rolling Stones. All these groups captured the musical interest generated by the Twist. Little Richard, the popular rhythm and blues artist of the fifties who had written hits for Pat Boone and Bill Haley, had traveled periodically in Europe with the Beatles and had influenced their style. At the height of their success the Beatles proclaimed, "We sing more African than the Africans do."

The Beatles, the Animals, and the Rolling Stones brought to America a high degree of sophisticated musicianship not normally found among white rock groups at that time. Even more significant, however, the English groups, who had the nation's attention, gave full recognition to having learned their music from the records of black American rhythm and blues artists.

Young white Americans, whose perception of the music had been distorted by the mass media, accepted the truth from the English; they adopted a purer form of rhythm and blues. It was then that the rock revolution began. Inspired by the rock revolution, young white Americans began to search honestly for the roots of what is commonly called rock music. At the end of the rainbow they discovered the blues.

"For commercial purposes," states Brownie McGhee, a famous blues guitarist, "people have changed the blues title, but they haven't changed the blues. I've been through five changes in my days—

country blues, corn field blues, city or urban blues, boogie-woogie, and rock and roll—and they all stand on the foundation of country blues. . . ."

McGhee's statement reflects the basic conclusions of my research: that rock and roll was initially rhythm and blues and that mass communications media really created the dichotomy between the synonymous musical terms. In 1954 rock and roll became a popular musical term because radio disc jockey Alan Freed wanted to popularize rhythm and blues under the name of rock and roll in the hope of getting young white people back on the dance floor. Motion pictures, television, and the press followed radio's lead in perpetuating the dichotomy.

My research leads me to view as invalid and without adequate support the attitude that some fundamental differences set rock and roll apart from rhythm and blues. Rhythm and blues has always been a music reflecting a wide variety of styles and allowing for wide individual expression. The African characteristics of antiphonal singing (call and response), sliding around and into notes rather than hitting them straight on, and playing with notes while expanding or contracting a phrase is very much the heart of rock music. If the African beat and rhythms were removed from rock and roll, the music would no longer rock. We must never forget that rhythm and blues was called rock and roll because that is what it made people want to do. In that basic sense, the music has not changed. It has only progressed, with valuable contributions being made by many creative and imaginative people from various backgrounds and subcultures.

The failure to recognize that rock is the cultural product of African-Americans represents the American custom of weaving history without the beauty of color. Mass media have only reinforced that custom. To admit that rock is based on rhythm and blues would not give respect, credit, and recognition to black Americans. Too many radio directors and television and film producers believe the theory that country and western, pop, rhythm and blues jelled together to form rock and roll. The mass communications media have succeeded in convincing themselves, along with the general American public, of the melting pot theory. That is only a smooth way of refusing due respect to black Americans for their creativity, because the society cannot accept a product as equal if its creators are considered inferior.

European music, of course, has affected the creations of African-

American music, but somehow the pendulum swinging in the oppo-
site direction has not been positively communicated via mass media.
Even if it were true that a combination of pop, country and western,
and rhythm and blues came together to form rock, as has been
conveyed in rock documentaries, the African impact upon pop and
country and western music is too often overlooked or missed en-
tirely.

What was called pop music in the early fifties is based partly on
imitations of Africans, beginning with the minstrel show, which
passed its tradition on to vaudeville. Al Jolson, Eddie Cantor, Sophie
Tucker, and others were all attempting to imitate portions of African-American music. Not to be overlooked are the significant roots
of American pop music, which go back to Stephen Foster, who
worked magnificently with a music form highly influenced by blacks.

With all due credit to country and western music and its creativity,
it too has been affected by the black experience. It is with a great deal
of respect that the honesty of Paul Hemphill's words from the *Nashville Sound* are quoted:

> All along, there were other influences working to change the music as the
> people began moving out of the hills and the tidewaters and the foothills of
> the South. The Negro, with a music all his own, wrought subtle changes; he
> taught them how to pick the guitar rather than merely strum it, and even
> today there is a term, "nigger-pickin,' " denoting the use of the guitar as
> something much more than an accompanying instrument. The Negro also
> taught them what is today called "country blues" and has been commercially
> successful through Negro performers such as Blind Lemon Jefferson and
> many folkpop stars of the sixties. And still other changes were wrought by
> early industrialization, migration to the cities, exposure to the traveling medi-
> cine shows with their Swiss yodelers and black comedians and Hawaiian
> bands, and the tent shows with their dancing girls and Irish tenors. Once the
> country boy went back home—from the city, from a medicine show, from a
> railroad trip, from a jail, from whatever—he took with him new song ideas
> and new methods for singing or playing them: the yodel, "nigger-pickin,' "
> railroad songs, the blues, the evils of the city, a new appreciation of the old
> homestead, the influence of jazz musicians he had heard on Beale Street in
> Memphis.[1]

So in essence what we do when we say pop, country and western,
and rhythm and blues combined to form rock is to come full circle
back to Africa.

Hopefully I have made it clear by now that Alan Freed, using the influence of New York City and the power of radio, merely changed the name of rhythm and blues, not its musical structure. And if rock is a music different from rhythm and blues, it is not the music Alan Freed was referring to but something different—not rock.

Black singers and musicians have a long history of developing new trends and styles apart from white musicians who, while studying the music of blacks, often omit African-American recognition. In the work *Black Rage,* authors William H. Grier and Price M. Cobbs address this point:

> Black musicians have always sought to express something uniquely black and express it in a way which leaves whites dumbfounded and excluded. No sooner have some whites learned the special techniques than Negro musicians develop a new, more difficult technique, and when that too can be shared by whites, another more complex idiom is developed. Any student of contemporary music can follow this evolution and will be impressed by the technical and theoretical developments black musicians have moved toward in response to the drive for a unique and ethnically singular method of expression.[2]

This constant exploration for new creative avenues is one of the primary reasons that rhythm and blues, or soul music, that blacks perform today is noticeably different from that of 1954, and equally so, the music the whites perform today when compared to their initial attempts to imitate rhythm and blues in 1954.

Mass media have not only brainwashed white Americans into thinking that their youngsters of the 1950s developed a new musical culture, they have left a desolate imprint upon the lives of Africans in America. Where they could have created positive concepts of black people by emphasizing their contributions, radio and television broadcasters have done otherwise in a host of ways. Therefore, it is the responsibility of broadcasters to correct the situation. The programing of music, the universal language, is an excellent starting point. It is inhumane for network television to perpetuate the absence of African-American musical programing from its schedule.

The time is long past for all Americans to know the contributions of black Americans. Guest appearances only "feed it to us with a teaspoon, throw it at us with a shovel!" Only broadcasting can rectify this situation.

The whole free world has rocked and rolled to the Twist, the Monkey, the Dog, the Jerk, the Watusi, and the Shake a Tail Feather. And yet it has failed to realize that these renowned dances

are rhythm and blues songs and choreography. It is time for white
Americans to look at black Americans' contributions to this great
nation and to identify black Americans with those contributions. If
this country is to succeed in peace, America must cease incorporat-
ing the black man's creativity into the American fabric at the same
time it rejects the black people.

Ask yourself now, "What is keeping the recording business a billion dollar
industry?" The answer is—rock and roll—the beat the Beatles rocked this
country with on their way to their first million dollars.

Who created this "beat"? The answer is—The American Negro because
none of the other immigrants brought it with them. The white minstrels who
blacked up and imitated the Negro slave didn't do it. What introduced the
"beat" to the world? The answer is Mamie Smith and the Jazz Hounds on
Okeh records.[2]

REFERENCES

1. Paul Hemphill, *Nashville Sound* (New York: Simon and Schuster, 1970), p. 117.

2. William H. Grier and Price M. Cobbs, *Black Rage* (New York: Bantam Books, 1968), p. 106.

3. Perry Bradford, *Born With the Blues* (New York: Oak Publications, 1965), p. 10.

PART TWO

On the Trail

of Soul Poets

THE FOLLOWING INTERVIEWS REPRESENT THE AUTHOR'S EFFORTS to document the black rhythm revolution as some of the music creators see it. These artists present a sample of many of the black contributors who are the foundation of the free world's most popular music. Some of the men represented here have been music creators and performers for the past thirty years or so. They are: Riley "B. B." King, songwriter, performer, and known as king of the blues; Brownie McGhee, a famous blues guitarist and songwriter; Arthur "Big Boy" Crudup, a famous singer and songwriter; Jerry Butler, a music publisher, recording artist, and songwriter: Dave Clark, a successful songwriter who has also produced a number of famous singing groups; and Jessie Whitaker, a songwriter and baritone for the famous Pilgrim Travelers gospel quartet.

In their own way and in their own words, they talk about their music, their songs, their recordings, other artists they have known throughout the years, and they expound upon their philosophy. All are unstinting in their praise of other performers they admire, and they reveal their own musical roots. To a man, they are enthusiastic and optimistic about the future of the culture, and they share what they have learned about music and show business.

These men are gentlemen, with deep pride and respect for the soulful experience. They are, after all, soul poets.

Riley "B. B." King

After World War II Riley King hitchhiked from his home in Indianola, Mississippi, to Memphis and got a job playing and singing the blues at the 16th Street Grill. To advertise where he was performing, young King secured a job on a new radio station, WDIA, and performed for ten minutes every afternoon without pay. Later, WDIA hired King as a disc jockey and called him "The Boy from Beale Street," and Riley King became known as "B. B."

B. B. King made his first recording in 1949 and by 1950 he was on top of the rhythm and blues charts with Lowell Fulson's "Three O'Clock in the Morning Blues." Today, Riley "B. B." King is recognized, as he has been among black Americans for over two decades, as king of the blues. He is a philosopher of the blues, and is as articulate a lecturer on the blues as he is a genius in performing them.

In June 1971 King made a personal appearance at Oakland University, a predominantly white college located on the outskirts of Pontiac, Michigan. Before his appearance there I interviewed him, along with Jimmy Brooks, a Detroit disc jockey and long-time friend of King's, and several members of the University of Michigan student newspaper.

U OF M STUDENT:	Did you close down the Fillmore East?
KING:	No, I didn't close it down. I was there the week before. I was there that Friday and Saturday, and I went back to help Albert [King] out on, I believe, that Tuesday or Wednesday or Thursday. It was one of those days.
U OF M STUDENT:	How did you find the crowd there, the people who came to see you performing in New York, as far as getting into the music you play, your blues and everything? Were they receptive, or how did you find the young people of 1971 that came to see you perform?
KING:	Well, I found them like this. Everybody was seated—when they mentioned my name, they stood up. That's the first thing. When they brought me onstage, everybody stood up. After my second number, they stood up again. My third number, they stood up again. In other words, I had about five standing ovations before intermission.

U OF M STUDENT:	I think that's enough said right there.
KING:	Okay.
REDD:	Has this happened to you—you know, the ovation—really the warmth—when you played what Lou Rawls calls the "chitlin' circuit"?
KING:	No, it had never happened. The first time I ever had a standing ovation in my life was three years ago, and I was at the Fillmore West in San Francisco. It had never happened. But since then I've had it happen a few times, which makes me cry every time I see it, because I'd never had it happen before that time, you see.
REDD:	Now, is Albert King your brother?
KING:	My father says no. My mother died when I was nine, and my dad tells me unfortunately I'm not related to any of the famous Kings. I wish I was.
U OF M STUDENT:	What was the importance of something like the 1970 Ann Arbor blues festival?
KING:	What was the importance?
U OF M STUDENT:	Yes.
KING:	Well, it was playing to people that had never heard it. And especially seeing the performers perform in person.
U OF M STUDENT:	How did you feel as a performer playing before a white audience like that?
KING:	I felt very good because I thought that they wouldn't have been there if they didn't want to learn something about it. And I thought that it was my job to try to do what I could to show them that there was some art in it.
U OF M STUDENT:	And you felt they got into the music the way you would expect a black audience to?
KING:	I really didn't have no expectations of how they would react to it, other than to listen, you know. I was hoping that they would listen. But I think of an audience as I do myself. I go many places to hear people that I didn't know

about, but I never put them up here. Nor did
I put them down there. I just went and listened. And later on, maybe in three or four
days, I decided that, yeah, it was okay. You
know, that kind of thing.

U OF M STUDENT: How do you get into the mood before you go
on stage to do a show?

KING: Well, I try and watch the crowd just a little bit,
and try not to listen to what I'm listening to
now [*The Patterson Singers*]. They've got the
people going out there now, and I'm trying
very hard not to hear it, you know. Because
that usually weighs on my mind very hard,
thinking about what all I have to do to try and
get people to listen to me and see if I can bring
them back up to the same standard at which
these guys are going to leave them. But I usually get in the mood in my room before I go
onstage, like we are doing now. And try to
throw every bit of it out of my mind completely. I probably, if we hadn't been doing
this interview, would have had my tape re-
corder on listening to somebody else. And
mostly some of the older things that was way
back. I hardly listen to many of the new things
unless it's a particular number by a particular
group that I like. But I usually won't listen to
the whole thing, just that particular number.
And after I listen to that, I always go back.
Now I buy records. I buy all the new records
that come out usually. But I pack them back
and I won't listen to them for three or four
years. That's when people stop playing them.
Then I'll go back and I'll pull them out and I'll
start playing them again, you know.

U OF M STUDENT: Do you feel that there's a point once you're out
there that things start picking up?

KING: Well, what I usually think of when I go out
there, I watch the people. I open up with "Ev-
ery Day I Have the Blues"—which is my

theme song. After that I try and see the reaction, if the people are ready for that kind, because it's usually up tempo a bit. After that, then I'll usually play following with "How Blue Can You Get". And the reason I do that is because it's got a little punch line in: Like "I give you seven children, now you want to give them back." The reason for doing that is to see if there's anybody ready to laugh, you know, if they really want some fun, you see. Or if they want something slow. And I can usually tell from the reaction of the people right then and there about whether to do another like that right away or to leave that and go to something else. And I usually—they're putting it on out there, ain't they? So that's the way I do once I'm on stage. I start to keep in my mind how the people are reacting Now most—I'd say ninety-five percent of the time it works. But the other five percent it don't.

U OF M STUDENT: How did you feel about the "Cook County" record?

KING: How did I feel about the record itself or recording there, or just the record?

U OF M STUDENT: No, the record itself.

KING: The same way I feel about most of my records. I feel that I made a lot of mistakes in it, but I think it's all right.

BROOKS: Well, B.B., I've talked with you several times. I've known you personally for years.

KING: Right.

BROOKS: As many times as I've talked with you and as many times as I've played your records, day in and day out, I've never asked you this: When were you affected by the big change from the old B.B. King? Was Hummingbird the first record that came out with the change?

KING: No, the old B.B. King started in '53 or '54, when I made songs like "How Do I Love You." Not "Darling You Know I Love You"

—"How Do I Love You." That was in '54. "How Do I Love You"—we did about eight tunes of that kind, of that caliber. That was the change of B. B. King then. That was in '54. I would think Hummingbird would be different from the other things. But the change actually started from the old B.B. King about '54. But the point still is, I didn't think of that then as a change that changed me from what I had been doing, with the exception of trying to let the people know that I am a little bit versatile, that I can do more than one type of thing. This to me seems to give the artist just a little bit more respect. You find that—I think one of the things that makes Sammy Davis such a great artist is that he can do so many things. And people tend to kind of give you a little more credit once they find you can do more than one thing, even though one thing is your specialty. And blues is mine. I don't think I can do anything else as well.

BROOKS: People have a tendency to, until they get used to it, like you say, people get themselves in a frame of mind where they're used to one thing. And when you start something new, when you're being versatile, showing that you can do more things, people become a little stagnant, kind of back away. Like the action on Hummingbird for a minute was nothing. But then it got into a beat, then began to really move.

KING: But it still was one of my big records. What I want to say is this. I don't know what other artists think of that. But the way I always think about it, I think of it this way. I was a disc jockey, too, and I used to play records a lot of times that I didn't like. I played them because people liked them. But I think of it this way. I used to introduce "Sweet Sixteen" sometimes to the public and say "Ladies and gentlemen, this is my new tune that I'm going to record." And when I'd sing it, some would say, "Aw, sing me 'Three O'Clock Blues,'" you know. So what I'm trying to say, you have to be your own man, use your own ideas, and put it out. You've just got to be the guy. It's just like putting out *The Sensuous Woman* or something like that, you know. You've got to just go ahead and do it and hope that the people will understand what you are trying to do. Do you follow me, what I'm trying to say? In other words, you can't ask the permission of the audience or the people to record a song. Because if you did, it's not going to be like a committee sitting at a conference where the chairman of the board has to talk to his staff. Because two thirds of the time they're going to vote you down. This is what I'm talking about. So you got to go ahead and make your own choice, do what you're going to do, and try to be creative. Because if you don't be creative, or try to be creative, then you never seem to move. It's just like a show, a radio show or anything else. If sometime you don't bring up something that's a little different from your competitor, you get lost. You get lost.

BROOKS: Hey, B.B., you got no competitor on this show. We're pegging for you.

KING: All right, okay. You know what I mean? So this is why I have from time to time tried one thing or the other, one thing or another. Sometimes it works; two thirds of the time it don't, but you still keep trying. Because if you didn't do that, man, you would get to the place where —if I had to sing just one song every night, every night, every night, and couldn't sing nothing else, it soon would get boring, you know. If you had to go to the same place every day and do the same thing—even jobs. Maybe you may be doing the same kind of thing, but not the same thing. Whatever you had to do today, if it's nothing but welding a tank, at least you finish this tank today, and you push that tank over, and you start on another one tomorrow. That kind of thing, you know. At least this gives you a little bit of relief in here, man. If you had to go and say hug the same woman every day at the same time, you know, every day at noon you got to go hug this lady, after a while you're going to be tired of hugging that lady. You'll wonder if you can't hug her at, you know, like two-thirty at night, or maybe eight o'clock in the morning. *(Laughter)* Do you understand what I mean? That's just like being in an institution or something, you know. And this gets to be a thing.

REDD: I guess one of the things that has always interested me is I've always seen the name "Jose" as a cowriter with you.

KING: That is just a fictitious name that the company used to claim a part of the song.

REDD: I see.

KING: But there was no one of that name that was with me at that time.

REDD: I see. That brings out another point, I guess, when artists break into the business, they are taken by the publisher into the company, into the business.

KING: Well, I'll put it this way: A lot of things you don't know when you first start, nobody tells you. *(Laughter)*

REDD: Okay, Kent records also seems to create a double release whenever you release from ABC. Is there a reason behind that of any significance?

KING: Well, I was with them from '49 through 1960 or '61—I've forgotten now—I think it was '60 —so I was with them for about eleven or twelve years almost. And we recorded many, many, many things with them. Of course, when I left them and went to ABC, the company I'm with now, they gave ABC a release of about eighty tunes that had never been released, you see. So I've been away from them now ten years, and, of course, what they do, most of the things that were recorded were recorded at that time like on four tracks, see. So it's very easy for them to take my voice and my guitar off and write new arrangements around it. But anybody that's familiar will know that it's the same song, or the same voice from a prior release, but they have to listen carefully because the new arrangement of the new happenings around some of them make them, you know, you have to really listen closely to tell.

REDD: That also makes you one of the most prolific writers around, doesn't it?

KING: Well, now, I don't know about that. *(Laughter)* Well, I don't know about that, but I do know that it hurts at times and then it helps at times, because the way it hurts is that if we've got a good record going, then they release one that is good, then it takes away the sales on the other one. But the way it helps, it keeps the company that I'm with now on their toes. *(Laughter)*

REDD: I've listened to what people call the Chicago blues, and I know you're extremely modest, but Chicago blues to me is B.B. King blues.

KING: Well, I like to see it this way. Most of the people that are in Chicago, what they call Chicago, wasn't born in Chicago. So a lot of them came from the same areas that I did. For instance, Muddy Waters, who I think is one of the greatest of greats, and the kind of blues that he does is from Mississippi. Let's see, Jimmy Reed is from Mississippi. I'm not familiar, but I think Howlin' Wolf is from Arkansas, I think, I'm not sure. But I know Muddy Waters is from Mississippi, and I know John Lee Hooker is from Mississippi, Otis Spann is from Mississippi. In other words, most of the guys that are there now that have made what they call Chicago blues are living in Chicago, but they aren't from Chicago originally, you know. So I would think that—well, even for instance Little Milton. Little Milton is from Mississippi, Ike Turner is from Mississippi—of course, Ike has never lived there much—but I know Little Milton lived around there, and Buddy Guy is from Louisiana. So most of the guys are either from the South or around the southern areas that came to Chicago and made it home. But I think one of the reasons for that is Chicago is, and of course has been, like Memphis used to be. It used to be all the southern people— not that I'm excluding Memphis as being a southern town—but I meant farther south, like the lower parts of Mississippi and all around. You know, like Alabama and the northern parts of Georgia, eastern parts of Arkansas, eastern parts of Texas—all these people usually would come in to Memphis, because Memphis was know as a blues town. What I mean by that, you could easily go in, you see, and get a job. Well after Memphis began to change, then the guys started leaving there. Leaving Memphis and going to Chicago was almost like leaving the United States and going to England.

REDD: Why is that? Because as I recall before you told me that WDIA opened up there, and it was probably because it was a very popular blues town. But then guys left and went to Chicago or what have you.

KING: Well, after a while, see, when rock and roll got to be very popular they stopped playing blues like they used to. There used to be—cause I was a disc jockey from '49 through about '52,

almost '53—and all doing the—well, like '48
—I think that's when the station first started,
which was the first black-operated station in
the area, in fact that I know of—and at that
time they played people like Muddy Waters,
T-Bone Walker, Charles Brown, Jimmy Witherspoon, John Lee Hooker, Joe Liggins, and
Roy Milton, Roy Brown. All these many people, man, was being played then. Then after
rock and roll got to be so big, then you—you
know. Like I don't blame people for going
with the trends, yes, but my God, Ford still
has one of their first old Fords around.
(Laughter) You understand what I'm trying
to say? In other words, a lot of things that
people call old become antiques and become
very valuable after a while, you know. So I
think they should be brushed off and shined up
every once in a while. So this was one of the
things that started to happen. Now we know,
or I believe in, each group or each flock stick
with its own, yes, but you don't exclude everything else. I don't think so, you know. So, what
has happened? Chicago has maintained some
of that. WVON and my friend Purvis Spann
will play some blues, you see, and we have
found—through my little research, I've found
that the my little research, I've found that the
music that we hear today—soul music, rock,
hard rock, and many different types of music
that you hear today—has been influenced by
blues. So I consider blues as a mother tree, and
many branches have sprouted from it. So it's
just like having a great-great grandfather that
was a slave. You know, people look at each
other and they start to think about it, and they
say to themselves, they say well like he was a
bus driver, or he was a truck driver, or he was
this, but he still was your grandfather. You
know, it's just unfortunate that he happened to

be born during that time of slavery. But you can't look at him and laugh at him, man, You know, like a lot of people have people coming in from the old country. Some of them seem to be a little bit ashamed of him because he don't speak good English or, you know, he don't act like we act. I'm trying to say and relate all this back to the blues. And this is what they did for some of us for a long time. People seemed to have been ashamed of us because we sang or played blues, you know. They'd say, "That ain't what's happening, man." You know. But Chicago didn't do it, so this is why I think Chicago became the Chicago that we blues singers love.

REDD: You've mentioned many times that T-Bone Walker and Lonnie Johnson were a part of your foundation.

KING: Yes, oh yes, yes.

REDD: And I guess your own cousin, or uncle, Bukka White.

KING: That's my cousin, Bukka White.

REDD: You've also mentioned another fellow that was a guitarist for Johnny Moore and his Three Blazers.

KING: Johnny Moore himself. Johnny, oh God, yes. Johnny Moore who just died, I think, last year —year before last. But there was others, see, like Charlie Christian, I liked. See, I liked jazz too. And then Django Rinehart I was crazy about. But there was many in between. As we mentioned a while ago, it wasn't only just guitarists. Now like Louis Jordan, I think, is one of the greatest showmen in the world. I don't think nobody surpasses him as far as being a showman. And then the way he plays his horn and the way he phrases on it. Oh, boy. It just makes chills run up through me, you know. Then there were other people, many other people; like, for instance, Jimmy Rushing, I think, is the greatest blues singer we've had since I've been alive, you know. Then there's Joe Turner. Of course, Jimmy Witherspoon. And you've got many of these giants, you know, I picked one that's been around a long time. But you've got many others. Now like for instance Lowell Fullson. I learned a lot from Lowell Fullson. In fact, my first big record, "Three O'Clock Blues," was written by Lowell. And I used to love him—I still do. He influenced me some but not as much as the other people I've mentioned. This is why you often hear me say Blind Lemon, because Blind Lemon was *the* thing, man. When I think of him, I think about here was a little blind man that wasn't hardly five feet tall and at that time born to a poor black family. You know he didn't have no education because by them being poor they wasn't able to send him to school and learn Braille, you know, anything of that sort. So here's a guy who had to get out on his own to make a living, and he did it, and I'm sure many people took him one way or the other. You know how people do. And when I think about this guy, man, and hear him sing, I almost cry. And I say now here's a guy that was recording when the recording industry just began. He didn't have no guidelines to follow. Look at me, man, I've got tapes, tapes of people, people, people, and here I can't play no better than I can. *(Laughter)* That's terrible. Isn't that awful? When there are, you know, books, books, records, records, you know, I could listen every day. And you know, here I am. Man, I feel real sad about that sometimes.

REDD:

I worked in Nashville with Morgan Babb, who was one of the original Radio Four, and he was telling me that when you recorded "Three O'-Clock in the Morning Blues" you really went into the studio to do a gospel or a religious number.

KING: Well, I had been singing spirituals prior to that, yes. But we did go in to cut what we cut. But I had been singing—maybe he knew that I had sung spirituals before I went into this. But we cut "Three O'Clock Blues" at the YMCA in Memphis. But that was about the ninth record that I had made. I had made eight before that—seven or eight records before that—and they had been pretty good sellers, but neither one of them had been a hit. I had never had what they consider a hit until "Three O'Clock Blues."

REDD: Musicologists now that are digging into the music and say there's a Texas blues, a Mississippi blues—do you find any real difference in that?

KING: Yeah, labels. *(Laughter)*

REDD: You mean blues is the blues.

KING: Blues is the blues. I just find labels. They say Mississippi blues, Chicago blues, Delta blues, White blues, Black blues. I find one—blues. But I do find, you know, some people play it better than others—like some whites, some blacks. I find a lot of people play it to me much better than I do. But all in all, when you boil it down, as far as I'm concerned, it's blues.

REDD: Is there a relationship between the blues and country and western music?

KING: I think so, quite a bit. You know, being from Mississippi, as I mentioned earlier, when I worked on the plantation, which I did most of my life, you know, until I left home, there wasn't many radios in the area. Only the bosses had radios, and I was a houseboy part time. And being a houseboy working around the boss's house, the only kind of music I usually heard was like country and western during the week, spirituals on Sunday. And, of

course, you started later in the forties to hear
a little jazz being played on the radio. So that's
all you heard. Now another thing, in the area
where I lived, you could look at the houses and
you didn't know who lived in them, white or
black. That's just how poor the area was. So
the only time you knew anything different you
had to look very close. You had to look again
to see if they was white, you see. You dig? So
I'm trying to say, in my funny words, that the
blues to us, was the same thing as country and
western were to the poor whites in the area.
Do you follow me, what I'm trying to say? So
we all had our story, but telling it in a different
way. Like maybe you speak French, and I
hardly speak English, but anyway when I tell
my little story, I tell it in my own tongue. This
is what I think was happening with them. And
with the exception—now please try and get
this if you can—a lot of the blacks in the area
not only were working hard and in a lot of
cases but felt cheated in many ways—in many,
many ways—he felt that a lot of time that his
woman was kind of goofing up from time to
time. Anyway, so a lot of cases—the whites,
their association wasn't as much as it was the
social bit of the black people. 'Cause the black
people were always together, getting together,
so it was very easy for a woman or a man to
cheat a little if they wanted to, and in a lot of
cases it was the only way some of them found
a little bit of extra enjoyment, you see. *(Laughter)* But in the whites, they had to be kind of
cooped up, because a lot of them didn't associate with the blacks, and there wasn't many of
the whites out in the area. So they always was
singing *to* their lady, and about how much
love there should be, and what have you. And
we cats was singing about what she did last
Saturday night, you know, that we didn't dig,

and that kind of thing. Do you follow me? So, in so many words, if one takes country and western music and really listens to it—really listens to it—and have a soul like the kind I've got, you'd be able to feel it. Like Hank Williams, man, when he wrote "Cold, Cold Heart," tunes like that, that carried me right back to my same old blues about "don't answer the door," and all that kind of stuff. 'Cause this is a guy hurting. He's hurting from inside. And "Your Cheating Heart"—many things of this sort are just to me another form of blues sung by other people. And they call it country and western.

REDD: You sang gospel starting off, and that perhaps is the least researched field of all. People hardly know Sam McQuary and the Fairfield Four.

KING: Oh, God, yes.

REDD: What can you tell us about that field?

KING: I can say that the only difference I find today singing my blues and going to church and singing the spirituals then was the words. Because I get just as happy, it feels just as good now, with the exception of the words. It's a beautiful feeling. I tell you what, to prove it look at there's Aretha Franklin, there's James Brown, there was Sam Cooke, and I could go on and name you many, many, many more that has got that feeling. Check them out and you'll find that they come from one of them Baptist or sanctified churches back there. *(Laughter)*

REDD: When we play in an African style, you know, we bend our notes and we slide into them, and we kind of waver a little off key. When you play your guitar, you bend the notes and you slide into things. Do you do that with a conscious effort from your culture, from your background?

KING: No, I'm not conscious of what I'm doing. It
                 just sounds better to me to do it that way. And
                 that's why I do it. You know, I'm not really
                 trying to, you know, make a mark here, a
                 mark there. It just, to me—it just—well like,
                 you know, many people have many sounds
                 when they're talking. For instance, I talk very
                 slow because I used to stutter very bad when
                 I was young. And I learned that if I want to
                 say something, to take my time and I'd finally
                 get a chance to kind of get it off and be able
                 to talk about it, you know, later on. But some
                 people will say a word abruptly, you know.
                 You know, Wham!, like that. Me—in order for
                 me to think within myself that I'm being able
                 to get you to understand something, I have to
                 really say it the best that I can and then maybe
                 look at you and see if I can see you getting it,
                 you know. Well, that's the way I am in my
                 playing. When I play a note, I want to get
                 every bit that I can out of that particular note.
                 And that's why it sounds better to me to kind
                 of pet it a little bit, bend it a wee bit. But it's
                 nothing that I'm doing, you know, that I'm
                 conscious of.

REDD: You mentioned a great many tremendous
                 blues performers, like Muddy Waters and so
                 forth. A lot of times I've found in lecturing in
                 schools that our youth know more about Ir-
                 ving Berlin—not to take anything from Irving
                 Berlin or Rogers and Hart—but what can
                 educators do to get our kids to know about our
                 songwriters?

KING: They can do the same thing that the white
                 youth has been doing for the last two or three
                 years, do research on it. Bring these people
                 out. Let them be heard. Talk about them. Give
                 the kid a chance to know whether he'd like
                 them or he don't like them. Bring the music
                 out. The music department don't have to play

Beethoven all day. They can play Duke Ellington, fine, beautiful. But then bring out some
Muddy Waters, some B.B. King, some John
Lee Hooker, and any of the guys—some Blind
Lemon. Show them where it started from,
bring it up. And then tell them: "You may not
like it because today, this decade of people are
much wiser than the people were back then,
but look at it and see where you got yours
from. See why you like to shake yourself a
little bit. It came from right back there with
that foot-stomping music, they called it." You
know, people used to do that. It used to be at
the bayous down in the areas where I came
from you could hear it on a Saturday night—
and they didn't have electricity—you could
hear the people stomping their feet. Sounded
like your school band drums, you know. You
could hear us way uptown. And you'd hear
some guy singing, and always with a big, fat
piano player—if you found one, fat in the
stomach, hanging over—and some funny-
looking guitar player sitting over next to him,
and more than likely a harmonica player, and
a few times some cat that had one of them old
rusty trumpets maybe, probably a saxophone,
but mostly an old rusty trumpet or trombone,
and once in a while a violin that some cat had
that looked like it had been out in the weather
for like ten or fifteen years. But if they would
do this, and give the kids, I think, a chance to
know these people. As I was saying a while
ago, maybe my great grandfather, who I know
was a slave, is nothing to be laughed at because
he's the cause I'm here, you know. And then
let the kids see for themselves. Sure we don't
want to take anything away from any of the
great greats. But all of these other people, just
like Shillinger said—Shillinger went all the
way to talk about W.C. Handy and many

other people in his book *The Shillinger System.*
He said there was this music—some people
use syncopation this way, others do it that
way. And he went all the way into Africa and
the Indians, and then he talked about Bennie
Goodman, when he was talking about swing
and all that, Artie Shaw, and the Charleston,
syncopation, and all this. But a little cat like
me, man, that didn't have no music in school,
and I get in this book, I learn so many things
that I'm ashamed of a lot of the things that I've
said over the years. And this I think would be
very good for the kids. Like, for instance, my
own kids. For a long time, man, like they said,
"Yeah, that's my daddy, but that stuff he
plays, oh my God." You know. Today they're
very proud of me, you know. I can walk up
and down, and my daughters get jealous if
anybody else comes up close to me. Course I
don't see them that often now, man. They
come up close to me and they don't even want
you to talk to me hardly. But it's only because
they know that they can be proud of me and
other people like me without being looked
down on by their friends or any other race,
because now they know that they have something that they can be proud of, because it's a
part of them. Just like the white youth now
I've found in a lot of cases know more about
a lot of the blues singers than I do. I didn't
know anything about Blind Willie McTell until about three years ago or four years ago.
Mississippi John Hurt, I didn't know about
him. I didn't know anything about him. But
now Blind Boy Fuller, yes, I knew of. Big Boy
Crudup, I knew, you know. I knew about—I
didn't know them. Sonny Boy Williamson was
my man, you know. I'm crazy about him. The
other Joe that was with Basie is a friend of
mine, too—but I'm talking about Big Joe, the

one that played the guitar, you know. And, of course, Brownie McGhee and Sonny Terry, well I knew about all of them. But a lot of the other people that's been coming up, I didn't know anything about them. But a lot of the white kids have told me—not the black ones, the white ones. The young white kids have told me, you know. Say, "Hey, what do you think of Leadbelly?" I've heard of Leadbelly, but I'd never listened to him. I really hadn't Josh White—yes, I knew. But I didn't care too much about Josh White because they called him a folk singer, and he wasn't singing my down home blues, so I didn't think much about it. But lately, you know, when I really started to doing research on him, I find that what the man was doing was great. But it still wasn't my kind of thing, so I have to respect him. There are many people in the musical groups that I respect, and you have to, because they're doing something you can't do. I can't play and sing like him, you know. But it don't mean that I'm just crazy about it, but I would support it and have to respect it.

REDD: When I saw you in Grand Rapids several years ago, you said you might be publishing some things, some B.B. King songbooks.

KING: Yeah, I've got two books out now. I have one B.B. King doing Billie Holiday, and then I have another one doing some of my own songs. And, of course, I'm working on a book now on my method of playing.

REDD: Beautiful, beautiful.

KING: Yes, that's what I'm doing now.

REDD: Now, why the blues explosion and why is B.B. King as big as B.B. King is today?

KING: I think this started back even with the Beatles, and nobody really realized it. The Beatles started people to listening—I mean the white area to listening and, of course, the hip black

area, you know, the young black areas. Now
I've had a black following that's been with me,
you know. Like when I was seventeen and
eighteen, I had people twenty and twenty-five
that was digging me then, and that have stayed
with me all through these years. We had a few
young black people, but rarely did we have any
whites that would acknowledge that they listened to us. I mean, talking about where people would know about it, you know. With the
exception of people in the musical industry,
you know, like record shops and, you know,
radio and things of that sort. The reason I'm
saying that is many of the white people have
told me lately, you know, in the last year or
two years, that they have listened to me all the
way back, from Randy's down at WLAC in
Nashville, and this was from '49 up. But they
never did say anything about it, so we never
knew. Because they didn't come to the dances,
and like you don't be there with a pencil marking that was a black one bought that one, that
was a white one bought—so you don't know
who's buying the records. However, I say I
think it started with the Beatles because they
started people not only to dancing but to listening to lyrics of the songs again. You know,
a long time back they did listen, but for a while
when rock came in people didn't think nothing
about it. You know, you could say anything as
long as the beat was there, people would dance
and they didn't care. Then the Rolling Stones
and many of the British groups started to do
the music then and they say to themselves "we
heard," you know, like Big Boy Crudup or
"we heard Muddy Waters" or " 'B.B.' King"
or, you know, "Jimmy Reed" or some of the
other guys "do this. That's where we got it
from." And so it was reimported back into
America, and then the white youth were buy-

ing it. But they also were listening and they
would hear these guys say that they learned it
from us. Do you follow me, what I'm saying,
man? So there's one thing I can say about our
home country. Everybody's usually hip, very
hip. So if somebody's saying that, you know,
like Muddy Waters is great, somebody in
America's going to check on it. They're going
to see why did this guy say he was great, you
dig? And this is what I think that happened.
They started mentioning my name and then
guys like Michael Bloomfield, Eric Clapton
from England, Peter Green from England,
Evan Bishop here at home, and guys like that,
which the white kids was already digging anyway, started to mentioning, "Yeah, you know,
like sure I play, but I learned mine from B.B.
King. I was listening to B.B. King." So then
the kids and the news media—everybody
started to check on B.B. King. Which, B.B.
King is doing nothing new that he hadn't been
doing all the time. That is, whatever trend of
music come out, I sing my same old blues but
try to use just a little bit of some of that background. You know, for instance, like when the
mambo was big, when calypso was big, I did
things like "Woke up this morning, my baby
was gone," things like that sort. Same thing
with rock and roll. When rock and roll came
out, I did several things with rock type background. Like soul, since soul has been out, do
a few things with just a little bit of soul touch
to it. And that's it. That's it.

Brownie McGhee

In 1939 Brownie McGhee met Sonny Terry, a blind harmonica
player, while hitchhiking in Burlington, North Carolina. It was the

beginning of a congenial friendship and musical association which, without contract, has remained active for more than three decades. During that time McGhee and Terry have delighted audiences the world over with their wide range of blues. It was because I had played some of McGhee"s old 78 rpm recordings from my family's collection as a kid that my admiration for him increased upon seeing his name as one of the original cast members of Langston Hughes' *Simply Heavenly,* which Dr. Thomas E. Poag produced for us at Tennessee State University in 1962.

The Sidney Poitier and Harry Belafonte television production of the "Strolling Twenties" left me in awe of Brownie McGhee's talent when he performed "Mister, Can You Spare A Dime?" Later I stumbled upon Sam Charter's book, *The Country Blues,* in which he documented McGhee as a major contributor to the blues and praised his guitar work. The Belafonte and Poitier movie sound track of *Buck and the Preacher* was superbly written and performed by McGhee and Terry, and offered additional and well-deserved exposure.

In February 1973 on the campus of Michigan State University I met Brownie McGhee and he shared some of his experiences with the blues, taught to him by his father in Knoxville, Tennessee. Brownie McGhee has written over four hundred songs, and today his primary concern is preserving the blues culture.

REDD: Mr. McGhee, what brings you to Michigan State University?

McGHEE: Well, they tell me they are opening up the first coffee house here and for some time, so we had the opportunity to come here and open it for them. What they call Mariah, I think, and last night was opening night, and it was a very good time.

REDD: Do you do these kinds of concerts around the country at college campuses often?

McGHEE: Yes we do, because I was just telling them how we sometimes go and spend weeks at colleges in Canada and upstate New York, and we stay right on campus. And we do a week there, and we are going from here to Austin, Texas, to some clubs, but then we're going in to Ohio to some schools.

REDD: Has your schedule with you and Sonny Terry always been this type of audience? Or how has it changed? What has made the change?

MCGHEE: There've been a vast amount of changes in it, because, being honest with you, when I left the South, there wasn't any place to play but what they call the "hole-in-the-walls" and "jook joints." There was no money there —you had to make your crowd, get there and play your music. But we migrated—I left Tennessee and come up to New York. I started street playing, there was a few clubs, and the war broke out. Then from the street to records, from records to clubs.

REDD: In the book, *The Country Blues,* the author, Sam Charters, says that there was a very peculiar kind of music in the mountains there around where you learned to play called "jooking." Can you talk a little bit about that?

MCGHEE: "Jooking" was a type of music that an individual created himself and brought out—what you might call self-styled. And I created a style of thing that from my area was called "jook." And that was what you might call between sanctified and blues. And we didn't just really have any set rhythm to go, we just jooked it out. We stomped on a beat. That's what we did. We played right on a beat, and sang on a beat and we jooked it out. And they got it from me because I had a little jook band in New York that followed me on up and I organized a jook band with a sanctified piano player, a tub beater, and a washboard band. And we just jooked it out for years.

REDD: You seem to be remembering some beautiful experiences as you talk about those times.

MCGHEE: Well, to remember them—I was born to remember, not to forget, because I wouldn't take a million dollars for my past. Yeah, because that's what I'm still living for: my past life, I wouldn't take a million, as I said, for my past because if I didn't have a past, I wouldn't have anything to live for.

REDD: What was it like playing those "hole-in-the-wall" joints?

MCGHEE: It was beautiful, I was just talking about it, you know, where they had chitlin struts, pigs feets suppers, and fish fries. Where you go to play, you make $2.00. Two dollars went a long way. If you got two bucks and all you could drink and all you could eat. Your friends danced and had a good time. It was marvelous, because two dollars was like two hundred today. I just regret that such things are not going now, so my kids could really experience what it was really like when I come along.

REDD: How many songs would you estimate that you have written, Brownie?

McGHEE: I have written—I have something down—like 400 originals, and I've recorded maybe in that area, something like that, but in the way of my repertoire is 700.

REDD: How does one remember all those songs? You must play a great deal.

McGHEE: A lot of people think that it's the songs to remember. It's the experiences that I have had. Daily happenings—whether they be good or bad—you don't forget things that happen to you and it's a steppingstone going forward, not backward. And I don't write from imagination—I don't dream up songs. And through my forty or fifty years of experience in this business, and in this life of mine, there's always something happening that I think people should know about. And that's what I write about. Of course, whiskey, women, and money has been the basic formula of blues, but in my blues, I use them as crutches. But there's something more. Most of my songs, deep down inside, is resentment, persecution. I want to know why certain things happen to me because my skin is black. I want to know why if I got a dollar I'm not accepted. But I don't press this on people in my songs, but deep down in, you'll find, when I get to it, it is a very socking hit—it's a hit. And that's what it is. Whiskey can be the title, but it's not what I'm talking about. That's to relieve my mind. Women don't treat me as bad as some of the songs think, but that's not it. People don't understand. Double entendre—that's what we write a lot of times. Whiskey, women, and money—they're crutches for me.

REDD: Were there some people that influenced you that we could talk about?

McGHEE: Oh yes, yes. Because if anybody says he wasn't influenced by someone, he's false. My father was a guitar player before me—not a professional guitarist—he was a hard laborer man, a common laborer, a part foreman. But his style of playing was his hard day's work. And I knew later on in years what he was singing about, but I loved to hear him sing because he didn't rhyme much. He was always singing about his hard day's work and how his hands were hurting and how his bones ached. It was very interesting to me, but it didn't seem like anything then. But later on I realized that he was talking about his suffering and what he had to do. Well, from that basically, I got my formula from my father. And my biggest influence was, I liked Lonnie Johnson. And I loved Lonnie. Temple Red. I like his style of things. Big Bill Broonzy. Lemon Jefferson—I listened to a lot of his things in those days, but my biggest influence was Lonnie Johnson. I like them all, but I never found anyone that beared on me like Lonnie's playing and his lyric writing. His songs and his lyrics impressed me most. And I got to meet him and I got to do a lot of things for him that I wanted to do for him and I got around with him and I found that he was a wonderful guy.

REDD: Mr. McGhee, could I just take that a little further. For a matter of documentation, just to say who Lonnie Johnson is and if it wouldn't embarrass you too much just to say what kind of relationship you later established with Lonnie Johnson.

MCGHEE: Well, 1948, I met Lonnie Johnson in a club in Chicago —Leadbelly, Mama Yancey, Papa Yancey. But I had listened to his records from my childhood, and I didn't think that one man could play guitar like that. Lonnie Johnson was from a big family down in Louisiana, and he used to have a brother that played piano. He played violin. His brother passed on, and Lonnie went on to St. Louis. And he won his first contest there, became known and started making records back in the way early twenties. He also was a jazz guitarist for Duke Ellington and the big bands at the time. He was a great jazz and blues man. In later years, well, Lonnie fell by the wayside, he got lost and I got in search to find him, and somebody

discovered him for me in Cincinnati. I was looking for
him to get him to make records again. He found that
people were looking for him and he moved to Philadelphia and started working in a hotel there. So somebody
come and said, "I heard you been looking for Lonnie
Johnson. I know where he's working." And I went to
Philadelphia and by some means or another. I ran across
a friend that was playing with him at this gathering
night and after night and he said, "Yeah, I can give you
Lonnie's phone number." I called up and got in touch
with him, and I got to meet him there. They got him in
to New York, and he made some records for Prestige.
That was the beginning. Then, he even went to King and
come out with a big hit record during that time, "Tomorrow Night," which brought him back into circula-
tion. Lonnie wasn't a baby, you know. It was 18—
something—when Lonnie was born. Lonnie was close to
seventy or eighty years old.

REDD: When "Tomorrow Night" was cut?

McGHEE: No, no. Lonnie wasn't that old. Lonnie was sixty or
seventy years old when he did "Tomorrow Night." But
Lonnie looked very good. You couldn't tell it. He didn't
show his age because he was a musician able to work,
and he had very good talent. And I thought he was the
greatest, and I always will say he was the greatest guitar
player; but anyway after that, he wasn't doing so well.
He lived in Pennsylvania—Philadelphia. And I knew
where he lived, and I'd go over and we'd have a little jam
session, and go out to clubs, to Sunday gatherings. And
I was in Canada, working, and somebody asked me did
I know a good guitar player. And I said, "There ain't
but one man that I'd recommend that I'd come here and
have a concert with, and that's Lonnie Johnson." He
said, "Do you know where?" and I said "Yes, I'll get on
the phone." He said, "Well, I'll send for him." So I said,
"Lonnie, would you come up and do a Sunday concert
with us? We got a ticket waiting for you." He said, "I'll
come, Brownie." So I sent for him to come to Toronto
from Philadelphia. He come up and people liked him so
he stayed there; and unluckily, we just got him a two-

year contract for a club there, and he got hit by a car, went to the hospital, had a stroke, lost the use of his left hand. His fingering, he thought it was coming back, and he had another stroke. And I was ready to give a little party for his birthday, and I got a message that he had died.

REDD: What year was that, Brownie?

McGHEE: That was 1971. Two and a half years in Toronto. He died there. I took him up there and he lived there four years. Every time I went to Canada, he was there. That was the last thing I ever did for him. But while he was sick in the hospital, I used to take him out of the hospital and bring him to my apartment—rent him an apartment in a hotel, and it was good for him, to sit around and talk about old times.

   I did some articles on Lonnie for some newspapers, some of the newspapers. That was my life. We had a lot of things. I hadn't cut any records with Lonnie, and I was working on some deals to make some records—me and him, Sonny, some more musicians.

REDD: I guess a thing that creates an empathetic feeling for me: you talked about the "hole-in-the-wall" places, or the chitlin' places that you used to play in, lamenting that those places aren't around for your children or our children to at least appreciate. What kinds of things do you think are necessary so that our kids really understand that whole era that people like Lonnie Johnson and yourself have created in terms of the blues?

McGHEE: They have got to be talked about more. They have got to be brought into the schools. It's got to be lectured on. What I'm working on this now is a grant. If I can get a grant, I'm going to do it myself. Because I don't think the black kids really know the source from whence the music comes in America, of the black people. And they have been taught that the blues wasn't anything. And they have been separated. Blues and spirituals has a barrier between them which shouldn't have been. And they have got to bring these stories together—religion and blues are actually happening in people's lives. Our people had to have something to cling to in slavery.

They had to hold on to an unseen guess. They were taught that. And the radicals sang the blues about realistic things of life. But as I said before, resentment of the way he was being treated. And the white man began to accept these blues, not as though he was being talked about, but as if we were talking about him through our woman—to him. And it seemed to be a thing of that's one way to get back at a man, at that time. And this is what was called blues. And blues just seemed to be what they might call the black sheep of the family, you sing that, but we gonna sing "Swing Low, Sweet Chariot." And I come up in that type of family, and when I was there, I had to go to church. But I could see a little further than that because I talked to some of the older heads and got my information from the real source. What is religion? What are y'all thinking about? What is the future? Are you really going to have to die to be happy? Or is there a happy place somewhere else? But they told me I knew too much, but I said, "No, I don't know anything. I'm asking you to find out. Should I stay here and pray with no knees in my pants, or should I get up and go somewhere and get me some pants? What should I do?" But they are saying, "Jesus's going to fix it." And I'd say, "He didn't fix it right. He's not fixing. He says help the man that helps himself. I got to help myself. He's in me. I got to help myself." So I migrated from there, and I said, "If everybody feels like y'all, I'll come back and die with you. But if not, I'm going on."

REDD: Brownie, have you gotten any good response, have you gotten any response, have you done any investigating on a grant to get this together in any way at all?

McGHEE: We're working on it. I must take something in to show for a grant. You can't just go in and say, "I want a grant." I'm going to have to spend some money on my own, to go around, like you are talking to me, I want to go and talk. There are a lot of old-timers still alive, musicians, and they'll talk to me because I know they will. But I first got to go and make this presentation and show them what I want to do. But I have to have some support. When you get a man to sit down and talk with you for days, you got to be able to help him some kind of way, because his time is important whether he's doing anything or not. And we need this on paper, and we need this in books, but I want the word from the men. I don't want people writing about them. I want them to talk about it, putting down what they say. This is what I want. I don't want me to write out something they say and me interpret my way. I want to get these fellows on tape, taken off a tape, put on pages, put in a book, so that we can go on from this and what happened and why did you quit, how did you start. I want to hear them say it. Such as Bukka White and Furry Lewis. All those old folks. They're still alive, but they won't talk to white people—they won't open up for them. But somebody's got to go and let them know what we're doing. This must be preserved, otherwise the culture's going to die.

REDD: Brownie, let me just go back a little bit and talk about your career, and ask you about Broadway. As I said once before, in undergraduate school, we were producing a play called *Simply Heavenly,* and I had seen Brownie McGhee because of some records that had been passed down to me from my folks and I never thought I'd get the opportunity to talk with you personally, but can you reflect just a little bit about *Simply Heavenly* and your role in that particular Broadway play?

McGHEE: Well, I can, because I knew Langston Hughes very well. And I was a street player at the time he was writing his articles for "Simple" in New York and I used to play bars late at night. And that's the time that Langston was going from bar to bar to pick up his lingo and his different things, and I think he was writing for the Pittsburgh *Courier.* Anyway, his article was running as "Simple." But he always—well, we communicated together time after time and during this play he was writing, it was mostly some things in that play resembled things that I was doing. Because I used to go in and play for bartenders at night and the guy said, "Get out of here, man." And I'd say, "Give me a drink." There wasn't nobody there, and I could play for the guy and sit down and drink free. And when the play come off, I was in *Cat on a Hot Tin Roof.* It was closing in Chicago, at the time: Burl Ives, Thomas Gomez, Ben Gazzara, and others in it. Langston called and said it'd be opening on Broadway, Brownie, and this role isn't that simple, but it was created for you. You wasn't on off-Broadway, but could you be in it?" I said I will be in, and it's closing in '58, and I'll come in. So they opened the first black play in twenty-five years—a black cast that opened on Broadway. And I had the part of Gitfiddle, and it was so much of me, the director said, "I got to change you, Brownie." But anyway, I just couldn't respond, the people that knew me and the type of guitar I play—I just couldn't stick to the script. I wasn't supposed to pick strong, but any way, *Simply Heavenly,* Gitfiddle, and I played the role then. Didn't do too bad. I think it was four months we stayed on Broadway. And I would like to do it again.

REDD: Sam Charters, who wrote *The Country Blues,* talked about jookin' and said that Jimmie Rogers, the father of country-western music, must have been playing something very similar to jookin' because that's what it sounded like to him. Is there a relationship—a direct, strong relationship—you see between country-western music and blues or jookin'?

McGHEE: There's a very close relationship. It's real close to western and blues. I used to play with the white blues musicians in Tennessee. And I didn't see much because the formula was there. But Jimmie Rogers was way back before my father's time and he was singing yodelin'. And if you ever notice and you ever compare it, when Jimmie yodeled at the time, Jimmie wasn't able to make any changes—turn, turnarounds. Our blues have a turnaround. I call it the same old diddle-dee-dee. Three, five, seven—if you want to call it that. But during the time that Jimmie Rogers was starting to yodel, most of his lyrics were railroad lyrics. There was a lot of black people on the railroad. All around the water tank. And I'd heard these lyrics in different forms; then Jimmie Rogers was the lucky one and he put it together and he just strummed his guitar and he made masterpieces out of it. His yodelin' come in from the turn. His yodelin' was really a turn on the guitar, which stood out. He made blue yodel number 10—one to ten. It might have went on beyond that, because we had every record that Jimmie Rogers made, because he was a very famous guy in the country around where I lived, in Tennessee, because those records come from Chicago mail-order houses—35 cents. And we never missed a Jimmie Rogers' yodel, and his lyrics—which I used to yodel myself, but anyway I was fleeced away from it because, you know, they called me imitating and I wasn't supposed to yodel. But I did yodel when I wasn't at home because it was an old field holler. We'd holler and we'd yodel like that too. And I still have a relation that yodels. Right now—I was just down there in July of last year.

REDD: Now, when you mean the field holler and the yodel, you mean that was sort of a personal identification when somebody was coming down the road or something?

MCGHEE: Well, when I first heard his first record, I didn't know what was going on. I just figured he did this to end a song.

REDD: Can I make an analogy between Jimmie Rogers of his day and Elvis Presley of his day?

MCGHEE: I don't know whether you could. Yeah, I think you could compare them in a certain sense, because, I'll tell you, music has steppingstones. It doesn't stay. I mean, the same thing can go on for years but you can't take a kid back forty years. But he can pick up where someone leaves off and go on. And that's the thing about it now, because Elvis Presley and Jimmie Rogers, I mean, Elvis Presley was very popular; Jimmie Rogers was very popular, too. So you can't say anything about it. I mean, Elvis Presley did, well, what you might call blues—rock and roll; and Jimmie Rogers did blues—blue yodel.

REDD: What was the change that took place in the blues scene around the end of World War II as compared to what the blues scene was like at the beginning or just prior to World War II?

MCGHEE: For commercial purposes people have changed the blues title, but they haven't changed the blues. I've been

through five changes in my days—country blues, corn
field blues, city or urban blues, boogie-woogie, and rock
and roll—and they all stand on the foundation of country blues—corn field music. What somebody called
"folk." All songs are folk songs, because they come from
just plain people. They have an origin and they all have
a background. They originated some place. But for commercial purposes, blues were black man's music, identified on the charts as the Sepia race. In later years, they
put it in to a rock and roll category, because everybody
felt there was something happening, but they first come
out of city blues. Electronics has added so much to the
blues field—it's stepped up. Only by the help of electronics—they're still playing the same thing, it's a little
louder. If you take those amplifiers off, you'll find it's the
same thing as when hand crankers were in style. But I've
been through five changes, and it's been for commercial
purposes. Rock and roll is the only time that the white
man got on the train of the blues. Otherwise, he was
afraid to touch it, until it was commercialized. Rock and
roll is just old plain country blues.

REDD: When you go around and play the blues, do you lecture,
           you know, during the time you're on campuses?

MCGHEE: When it's time and we have time. Mostly in California.
           I teach in California, but I haven't been teaching for the
           last two years. They get grades on that, and the type of
           music and the variations and types and when it made the
           changes, in the twenties. I used to do it, but I don't much
           now because they don't seem to have classes for it.

REDD: Brownie, where are those classes that you'd be teaching
           in California?

MCGHEE: I'd be teaching up in Idlewild, California, around
           U.C.L.A. Students would come up and study and lec-
           ture and write notes and things on what I did. I teach
           up there may be two weeks.

REDD: Have you ever gotten any invitation to do this kind of
           thing—to teach, to lecture—at what would be called
           black colleges?

MCGHEE: Black classes. Yes, up in Washington—Pullman, Wash-
           ington, and up in Seattle. We are now trying to find

openings also in Oregon. They're trying to have some heavy black classes up there. And we're trying to work something out with my schedule for me to get in at least a week at each one of these places. And if I can arrange it, where we can get in, maybe do a concert—maybe four or five days of just lecturing to classes, which we did in New York for quite a while, a number of years.

REDD: What would you like to say as a matter of historical record, if we might say, to all the things that you've been involved in and your hope for the culture that you've helped to maintain and to develop?

McGHEE: I can say this and I stand on it: Blues'll never die. It's gonna live in the form that the blacks see fit for it to live in. They won't go backwards; they'll go forward. They'll have problems, too. I hope they write about it and sing about it.

REDD: One final question, and that is last year I picked up an album and there was a song with you and Sonny Terry which was called "Look Under a Hood." Can you explain that?

McGHEE: Yeah. That's a comparison between a prostitute—a New York prostitute—and an automobile. I had a conversation with a prostitute, and she was trying—as a John—Did I have any money? Her motor was missing. She hadn't picked up anybody that day. She was doing bad. She didn't look bad; she just wasn't able to pick up anybody. So I went out and did this platter on that and I just sing, "Your motor must be missing. Let me check you out. Let me look at you and see what's wrong—what's going on." It was really a comedy. It's a comparison between a woman and a car. But it's really a prostitute—a conversation with a prostitute. And that's what I did. I don't say it, but anyway, when I talk about it I was on Broadway. At that time, I was brainwashed to death. I wouldn't go out without a tie and a suit of clothes on when I first come to New York, but otherwise I looked pretty good—no money. When you're walking down 42nd street, anybody will challenge you with a suit on and shoes shined, a white shirt and a black tie. But anyway, I got a lot of my gimmicks from that. And

I just figured that was about as close as I could get to it without just saying the natural thing.

REDD: There's also a very philosophical song called "Love, Truth, and Confidence."

McGHEE: I used to be a Bible teacher in the Baptist church, and this was one of my greatest things—a comparison between love, truth, and confidence. These are people— really people. Love, truth, and confidence. Without love —love is nothing, truth is nothing, without confidence. And it'd take me a few years to get the story down to where I could say it on records and in song. Basically, I usually keep everything that I start on. I simplified it down to—I really like the story, because it was beautiful. It was a long, long story.

REDD: Do you think there is a poetry of Brownie McGhee and Sonny Terry?

McGHEE: Yeah—I have it myself. I have thirty-five years of scrapbook, which is worth lots of money. I don't know how much, but I won't let it out of my hands. And everything I have is in poetry form. All of my songs are in poetry form. Maybe on brown paper, or newspaper edges, but I still have it. And the only thing I have to do is just publish it, that's all. But I just haven't. I'm working on it. I'm being honest with you—I'm working on it. But I don't want to give up what I'm doing now.

REDD: What can we do in the broadcast field, the education field, to assist you in the preservation of what you're trying to do?

McGHEE: It's to get more of it on, and without goofing it up— without it being adulterated. That's what I don't like. I don't like my songs to be adulterated. I don't like for them to take out stanzas and verses which mean something, and say this is not fit. It's simplified, it's stripping it of something. That's why I don't do much. I only go places and sing songs where they let me sing my songs. Once they listen to it, there's nothing vulgar about it. It's just really truth. That's all blues is: truth. Some people can't stand truth.

REDD: I guess an interview wouldn't be complete to ask you how you met Sonny Terry and how that came about.

McGHEE: Hitchhiking. I was hitchhiking. As I said, we wasn't put
together. Back in the thirties—late thirties, '39. Burlington, North Carolina, I met Sonny Terry and Blind Boy
Fuller. Fuller was feeble, sick, and I didn't know that at
the time. And we come up to Chicago to make records.
Fuller got sick, and I started to write him a song:
"Please, Mr. Fuller, Don't Die" and he died before I
finished the song, and they asked me would I write "The
Death of Blind Boy," and see what I could do. And I
wrote "The Death of Blind Boy Fuller." It was accepted
by Okeh records. And after that, I met Sonny and we
just—gentleman's agreement. No contract between us.
We're just two individual artists that met, and we pooled
our talent. We haven't changed that. He plays what he
wants to on stage and I support him the best I can. I play
what I want to play and he supports me. We've been
together thirty-four years. They wonder what is the formula to it—that's it. You never can change a man.
Don't take him out of his bag. Just give him all the
support you can in his bag, and he'll go on and on.
That's the formula to it. I don't try to pull him to what
I'm doing. He can't pull me to him. We just support one
another and that's it. It's congenial. It's what you might
call a friendship that has no ending.

Dave Clark

Dave Clark has worked in every phase of the recording industry.
He has produced such famous groups as the Dixie Hummingbirds,
the Mighty Clouds of the Joy, and the Sensational Nightingales. He
is presently producing the Rance Allen Singers. During his career he
has produced nineteen million seller recordings.

At the same time, Clark has created a reputation as an outstanding
and successful songwriter. Perhaps his most famous song is "Why
I Sing the Blues." He has been a songwriting partner of both B.B.
King and the great Don Robey.

Presently Dave Clark is head of Gospel Truth, a division of Stax
Records in Memphis. He has lived the great range of life, yet he

remains young in mind and spirit. And of black songwriters, the foundation of the big beat music, Dave Clark knows them all.

The following interview with Clark took place at his home in Detroit, Michigan, in August 1971.

REDD: Mr. Clark, how would you define the "blues"?

DAVE CLARK: The blues, I would say is the truth, and the truth is gospel so the blues is gospel, and gospel is the truth and truth is what you think is right. And together with a feeling and that anything that you'd find in most black people is found in the blues. Now for years people have looked at the blues as a thing where a man is leaving his woman or his woman is putting him outdoors, or a man is mad at his woman, and a man is catching his woman cheating or a woman catching a man cheating. But the blues is a different thing. When you walk down 12th Street you see the blues, you hear the blues. When you walk down Central Avenue in Los Angeles you hear the blues; when you walk down 125th Street you hear the blues. And when you walk down Auburn Avenue in Atlanta you hear the blues.

REDD: That seems to me to be a very good description of why you wrote "Why I Sing the Blues."

CLARK: Yes, it is because the blues is many things, if a man goes to work in the morning and looks down the assembly line and sees his work piling up; he works hard all day. He goes home to a house with the doors hanging off the hinges, the refrigerator done quit working, and no heat in the building, the rats ate up part of that last loaf of bread, man, that's the blues.

REDD: How long have you been writing blues?

CLARK: I been writing blues now for about thirty years.

REDD: Over those thirty years who were some of the tremendous black writers that you have known?

CLARK: Most of the black writers I've known, the greatest black writer of all I would think would be Duke Ellington, because he wrote blues, he wrote classics, he wrote operas, he wrote symphonies, he wrote them all.

REDD: You mentioned one black writer that is perhaps not known well at all but has probably five hundred published tunes, Rose Marie McCoy.

CLARK: Yes, she's not known among the black people, but in the recording industry and the music industry everybody knows Rose Marie McCoy. Because Rose Marie McCoy has become a fabulously rich woman from writing.

REDD: Who are some of the other greats that you mentioned earlier, people like Chuck Willis?

CLARK: Chuck Willis, Willie Dixon, right here in Detroit— Holland, Dozier and Holland . . . Gamble and Huff, these are younger writers, but they are great writers. Van McCoy, Aretha Franklin, she's a great singer and a great writer.

REDD: Why do you think that we, the people, the everyday person on the street does not know the Chuck Willises, the Rose Marie McCoys, like we know Irving Berlin or Rogers and Hart?

CLARK: Because Rose Marie McCoy, Chuck Willis, and Rogers and Hammerstein, they have all had exposure in the world. And we have helped this exposure; the people have been singing our songs, of black artists. And up until the later years a very few black artists played the best part, a very few black artists were even played on Top 40 radio.

REDD: So it boils down to that exposure?

CLARK: Oh, yeah.

REDD: Are you aware of the amounts of money, or the sums of money that are paid for a song being aired over national television?

CLARK: Oh, yeah, now when you say a song being aired over national television, now what do you mean, do you mean paid in performance?

REDD: Paid to the writer of that song?

CLARK: Oh, sure, millions and millions of dollars.

REDD: Do you think the black songwriter is getting his share?

CLARK: The black songwriter today is getting his share because he has woke up, he is a BMI writer. BMI or ASCAP, they are the ones to do the collecting from the networks.

REDD: Do you find that when black artists get on television they sing songs by black songwriters?

CLARK: Well, most black songwriters when they get on television today, if they sing a song they gonna have to sing what they know and what they know is by black artists.

REDD: I see. Who are some of the writers that you considered fine writers that perhaps have not become successful, but are good writers?

CLARK: Writer Joe Scott, even Willie Dixon. Of course, in the later years the English groups have been doing Willie Dixon's songs. Here at home you mention Willie Dixon, and they say, "Who is Willie Dixon?" And you pick up a Rolling Stones' album you might see three of Willie Dixon's songs; you pick up a Beatle album you might see three.

REDD: In my general observations, I've come across the name D. Malone and D. Malone, from my observation of records that I play has probably written more songs than any other songwriter that I've ever known. Who do you know as D. Malone?

CLARK: D. Malone is a collaboration of writers. I might be one of them, Joe Scott, Don Robey, Edrick Murchinson—any number of writers is D. Malone. It's a sort of a writing corporation.

REDD: Well, that explains why D. Malone is perhaps the Shakespeare of soul music. Of course, Don Robey is a fantastic writer.

CLARK: Oh, yeah, he writes some things.

REDD: "I'm Pressing On" was one of the things that Don Robey wrote.

CLARK: A gospel writing, yes. Don Robey has made a tremendous headway in gospel and blues. Like today you have a young black executive down at Stax Records that's making a great headway, Al Bell. Now, he's the vice president of the company, executive vice president of the company, and yet and

still he's one of the top producers and one of the top
writers down there.

REDD: What would you say is the contribution of all those
              writers you've known over the years, black song-
              writers that you've known over the years, to the
              present status of western music?

CLARK: Of western music?

REDD: When I say western music I mean that music which
              is popular in the Western Hemisphere that we tend
              to call rock.

CLARK: Eighty percent of all music in the Western Hemi-
              sphere is black-orientated. See, today if you hear a
              Rolling Stone song or you hear a Beatle song, if you
              listen close you'll hear some Chuck Berry, you'll
              hear some Bo Diddley, you'll hear some Muddy
              Waters, you'll hear "us." The record and the enter-
              tainment industry today is a billion dollar industry.
              And the black man has made the greatest contribu-
              tion to the industry, and he has received less than
              two percent of it.

REDD: Can you explain that?

CLARK: Yes, I can explain it. In the beginning, you take
              when at the beginning of the recording era, way
              back when you had artists like Big Maceo, Big Boy
              Crudup, Memphis Minnie, even Muddy Waters,
              B.B. King earlier, we had contractors that would
              come out, go all through the South and across the
              country, and record the black artists, give them $50
              for a wire-recorded session. He got the tunes that
              we had and everything for the $50. So when the
              tune was published they had the white man's name
              on it; when the records was made, he got all the
              royalties. This fellow didn't know his business. But
              it's a new day, you know the young fellows come
              a long way now—they know where it's at!! You
              can't get a young fellow today to sing you a song
              now unless he's got a copyright.

REDD: So that the publishing end of the business is really
              where the money is?

CLARK: That's where the money is, in that publishing end.

I never mentioned it, but I gave away fifty hits before I found out I could get paid for them. I thought I was just doing something for a hobby. I was glad to hear somebody sing my song, and we were just singing that white man rich.

REDD: So the big companies are really here because of the black man's talent and creativity?

CLARK: To show you how, in the forties one company had twenty million sellers by black artists. And out of those twenty million sellers the artists themselves didn't receive a million dollars.

REDD: In knowing my record history as such, in the records that were played it sounds to me like it was one of those labels that included Louis Jordan, Ella Fitzgerald, and Billie Holiday.

CLARK: Billie Holiday, Buddy Johnson, many of them.

REDD: You mentioned Buddy Johnson.

CLARK: Buddy Johnson is a great writer. "Since I Fell for You," "Be So Glad When My Man Come Home," and all those tunes.

REDD: How do you feel? You've been in the business thirty years writing songs, you've written great songs, and in my time, in recent times you've had some tremendous hits. You have a fast upcoming record now with B.B. King, "Ghetto Woman," but out of all of that effort you were successful, but those other friends of yours, great writers that you've seen that had great talent but did not get anywhere near their share of the money, which I'm sure you have not gotten from what you just said. How do you feel after all of these years, having known what black people have contributed to this country?

CLARK: Well, here's one thing, there's some bitterness you know, but then, too, you pay for your mistake, and the black man that I don't feel sorry for is the black man of today who walks into one of these publishing companies and hands his tune to the publisher to give half of the rights and everything else with one of them one-half percent contracts. It was a matter of ignorance, we just didn't know, and for years the establishment did a good job of keeping us from finding out. Until guys like Benny Benjamin, who is one of the greatest writers of all time and one of the great publishers of all time, until he walked in there and opened them doors, and became a member of ASCAP and started telling other writers about it. Until them fellows came along, Rudy Toombs and Henry Glover, until them fellows came along, we just didn't know. Like I started individuals in record promotion, by being in records and being in around record companies, I was able to find out earlier what was happening and I started pulling coats. It's pathetic, but it's true.

REDD: You mentioned Henry Glover, Rudolph Toombs. Of all the materials that are around and you were mentioning earlier about the truth and in fiction and so forth, but I would suppose that each of these lives that you have talked about as a writer is really a beautiful story within itself to be told.

CLARK: It is, it's a beautiful story, just like I was talking to you earlier about the blues and how it has affected the black man and about how we have been fooled about the blues like we have about black history. For years the plantation owner would tell the black man "don't sing them dirty Blues" because you were singing the blues about him. That would be your only way to tell him that you knew you were being mistreated; he wanted you to sing about them golden slippers and them pearly gates, and things that were going to happen hereafter, but he didn't want you to sing about nothing that was happening now, he didn't want you to sing about that mule you was plowing.

REDD: You mentioned earlier, and I was saying, too, that you really explode that stereotype of a blues writer, you are very articulate. What is your background? I said I wasn't going to ask you who Dave Clark is, but I have to.

CLARK: My background is a story. My background takes a lot of time. First, I started music at an early age

while I was in college, in Lane College down in
Jackson, Tennessee. I had the first band to play a
black radio commercial program in the South. To
start off with, in this band I had such musicians as
Ray Nance, Hank O'Day, some of the tops, they all
were students at Lane at that time. And after college I started out as a writer, not a songwriter, as
a columnist for *Downbeat* Magazine, the first black
one that they hired. I wrote a column called "Swing
Row Is My Beat" and I was doing research. I did
all the research on the King Oliver story, which
was one of the things that made *Downbeat* a great
magazine. From there I went into promotions, and
from promotions into writing, and I stopped playing music and started concentrating on writing.

REDD: A lot of the people that are institutions and legends
today are there partly because of the promotions
you did early in their careers.

CLARK: Oh, yeah, well I promoted a lot for the late Jimmy
Lunceford. I was the first promotion man he had,
and after Jimmy Lunceford, I was hired by Joe
Glazer to do Billie Holiday, Louis Armstrong,
luckily they all happened to be on the Decca label.
Then I supported Buddy Johnson, Ella Fitzgerald,
Chick Webb, also all on the Decca label. And then
later I became fascinated by the record business
and I went to work for Decca in their Chicago
record plant. Recordwise, I had all the experience
in records, from the plant to actual production. I
worked in the plant as a presser, from presser to
quality control to making masters, in fact, I did
everything in record business promotions, producing . . . And it's been the record business with me,
period, through the years.

REDD: In the King Oliver story that you wrote, I hope that
at this point I do not have King Oliver confused
here. But did King Oliver fall to poverty after his
reign?

CLARK: In his later years he died without a nickel in a little
cheap hotel in Columbus, Mississippi. King Oliver

was the man that invented the mute that all trumpet players use today. He took a plunger that we use, a bathroom plunger and hooked it over a Coca Cola bottle and made a mute out of it. He invented the mute that all trumpet players use today. King Oliver brought Louis Armstrong out of New Orleans. King Oliver was the first writer that wrote a score for jazz music. King Oliver was one of the all-time greats, but yet and still the present day-generation has never heard of the name King Oliver. That's what I was telling you about our black history. The kids today know nothing about these people. But they tell you about Booker T. Washington, and he's in the man's book as a great man. Because if it was left up to him, we'd all be tilling the soil right now.

REDD: What would you think would guarantee that writers like B.B. King, Aretha Franklin, Chuck Berry, Willie Dixon, yourself are not lost in the shuffle of history like King Oliver, Blind Lemon Jefferson, or Jimmy Cox?

CLARK: Well, they won't be lost in history for the simple reason that the young black artists are together, they are keeping up with the time and the only way that you can really learn about black history is to read black fiction, because the boys that write black fiction they don't pull no punches, they don't hide anything. If you're good, you're good, if you're bad they tell the story. If my kids don't read anything but about all the good things in the country and never know about the bad, when he walks out there in that world he'll be in a whole bunch of trouble.

REDD: Do you think that our music, black music, should be taught in the public school system?

CLARK: In all systems . . . Because you see it's basic for all the music today, man, if you gonna teach it, teach the basics of psychology, teach the basics of sociology and you teach the basics of everything else, why not teach the basics of music? You're going to school for orientation why not orientate in music?

REDD: Who is Pearl Woods?

CLARK: Pearl Woods is one of the greatest young singers and writers of her time. Pearl has written tunes for Ray Charles, the Drifters, Ruth Brown, Nancy Wilson, Bobby Bland, everybody.

REDD: What would you say to black people having any opportunity and taking this opportunity to say it to black people concerning that field in which you are involved?

CLARK: The first thing, if you are a writer you have got to believe in what you are writing, and before you give it away and sell it, explore it, see what the possibilities are. First thing to do is to get a copyright. That's where we've been making our mistakes. Just tell them young writers to keep it together. When I say keep it together, I mean keep it to yourself, get a copyright, and then sell it.

Arthur "Big Boy" Crudup

Arthur "Big Boy" Crudup is perhaps the classic illustration of many black artists who have contributed so much to this nation's musical heritage and yet received so little. He recorded nearly eighty songs for Bluebird and RCA records between 1940 and 1956. During that time he became a well-known and popular black recording artist. As a creative writer, he composed "Yonder Wall," "Rock Me, Mama," "Mean Old Frisco Blues," and "My Baby Left Me." However, Crudup, like many other black recording artists was poorly paid.

Leaving Forest, Mississippi, in the late 1930s, Crudup moved to Chicago and found it necessary to support himself by playing his guitar and singing in the streets. It was on the streets of Chicago that he and Lester Melrose met. Melrose, a publishing executive, got the singer a recording contract, became his manager, and billed him as Arthur "Big Boy" Crudup.

On October 7, 1947, Crudup recorded one of his many songs, "That's All Right, Now, Mama." Seven years later, Elvis Presley, trying desperately to find a groove during his first recording session for Sam Phillips, finally drew upon Crudup's "That's All Right,

Now, Mama," and successfully launched his recording career.

Now in his sixties and living in Exmo, Virginia, Crudup travels throughout the States, playing mostly to white audiences who have discovered the blues idol of their own superstar, Presley. In 1972 RCA Records, in the midst of the blues revival, released an album in tribute to Arthur "Big Boy" Crudup and entitled it "The Father of Rock and Roll."

The following interview with Crudup took place in March 1973 at East Lansing, while the famous artist was making personal appearances there.

REDD: You are legendarily known as "Big Boy" Crudup. How did that come about?

CRUDUP: Well, when I first started recording records, why, everybody wanted a nickname. And at that time I was a pretty large fellow—I was weighing about two hundred and twenty-five pounds—and they started calling me "Big Boy."

REDD: You recorded with RCA Records. Were you acquainted with the late Steve Sholes at all?

CRUDUP: Well, I first started recording records with Bluebird, and then, after the Bluebird was transferred over to RCA, that's when I met Steven Sholes.

REDD: The Bluebird label goes back quite a way in history itself. Can you tell us a little bit about the Bluebird label?

CRUDUP: Well, I don't know too much about it, because from 1940 —that's when I first started—and '42, why then RCA took it over. And I then was transferred from there to RCA, and, therefore, I don't know much about the Bluebird label, because I was just a young blues singer in the field at the time, see. I'd been there about two years.

REDD: Many times recordings were made by blues singers in the field, and in talking with Dave Clark—who used to write some things with B.B. King—he says that many of the times recordings were made in the field and that was just about the extent of the financial reward some of the blues singers received.

CRUDUP: Well, he's right about that, because there's many a one have made my numbers, and I haven't received any money from it. I've had several people make them, but I haven't ever received any money yet.

REDD: Mr. Crudup, do you have any idea how much you would have received had you gotten proper money?

CRUDUP: Well, from what I learned from first one disc jockey and another one, they tell me if I'd have got my proper money, that I would've been one of the wealthiest colored fellows in the United States; but I didn't get it.

REDD: Can you relate some of the songs that other people have recorded that you have written?

CRUDUP: Well, B.B. King did "Standing at My Window"—I did that; and "Rock Me, Mama"—I did that one; and Elmo James did "Dust My Broom; Hand Me Down My Walking Cane"—and I did that. "Yonder's Wall"—that's the name of it—"Yonder's Wall." Then Elvis Presley, he made three or four numbers of mine: "That's All Right Now, Mama," "Who Been Fooling You," and "My Baby Left Me." And he got rich off of it—got to be a millionaire—but I never received any money.

REDD: Have you been able to establish what element within the entire field, whether it's publishers or recording companies, or just what, that has been the holdup of your receiving the financial reward?

CRUDUP: Well, at the time, I had a manager—Lester Melrose. And Lester was the kind of a man who wanted it all for himself, I suppose. And he would tell you he would do one thing and he'd never do it.

REDD: When you were recording with RCA, were you properly paid by RCA?

CRUDUP: I was paid by Lester Melrose. I would go and record the numbers; then Lester Melrose would have a contract made out and everything, and I was getting so much a session, and my royalty statements came through Melrose. But I wasn't paid directly from RCA.

REDD: Getting back to Steve Sholes. Most of the writers that I have read say that Elvis Presley is a carbon copy of "Big Boy" Crudup. Did Steve Sholes, do you think, understand that when he signed Presley away from Sun Records.

CRUDUP: I don't know whether he did or not. I couldn't tell you, because I've never had any talk with Presley, and I've never met him. And if he'd walk in here now, I wouldn't know him from anybody else. And so, at the time that he made his first number of mine, I was managed by Lester Melrose. And so, now, I don't know whether he and Steve Sholes knew anything about it or not. Course, I figure that Meldrose did, because I told him when I heard the number about it, and he says, "I'll look into it." Well, he never did look into it. And so, now, whether Steve Sholes knew anything about it or not—I don't know.

REDD: How do you look at Elvis Presley in relationship to his initial beginnings in terms of using "Big Boy" Crudup's music? And I guess I would have to relate that to never getting in touch with you, not even after all these years.

CRUDUP: Well, I don't feel bad about him. I don't know him and then after not knowing him, why then he did just the same thing that other people have done. Why, when B.B. King made "Rock Me, Mama", he didn't get in touch with me. And when Elmo James—who was a friend of mine—made "Dust My Broom"—he didn't get in touch with me. And then some others made the number of mine —called "My Baby Left Me"—they didn't get in touch with me. They gave me the credit for the song. But no one got in touch with me and wanted to know would it be all right with me to make the song.

REDD: So there is no animosity that you have against Elvis Presley?

CRUDUP: No. Not against either one of them. They're all right with me.

REDD: Were there times in your career that you felt like, "Well, maybe I had better give it up," and then you started all over again?

CRUDUP: From the time I started up until now, I never felt like I ought to give it up. But I did quit from making records on this account: I wasn't getting the money that I should. And I always feel like if a person is working on a job, regardless of what it is—if it is farming, sawmilling, or railroading—if he's got to have two or three other jobs to make a living, he might as well quit one of them because he's not getting anything on it. And that's why I quit making records; I wasn't getting enough out of it to live. I'd had to go make some records, then go back

South, go on the farm, work railroad, cut pulp wood, work for the city, play music Friday night and Saturday night to try to take care of my family, and was supposed to be a musician and a record star. And so I just quit it. I found out all the money was going the other way and I wasn't getting any. And the jobs that I was doing, after I'd go make the records and come back, why that was the job I was supposed to be more interested in, but I was more interested in the record business, so I just quit. I quit in '55 and stayed quit until '62.

REDD: What brought Arthur "Big Boy" Crudup back?

CRUDUP: Well, Bobby Robertson, at the first beginning. I don't know how he got in touch with me, I don't know who told him where I was, but I got a couple of telegrams from him, and then I got a letter or two from him. And he wanted me to record some numbers for him. Then I recorded those numbers for him in New York, for the Fire Record Company. And after I recorded them, why everything so he said, would be all right. "In a few weeks, you'll be drawing money." But I never did draw a dime, no more than what I got from the recording field. And so, I quit again. Then I made some numbers for Delmar Record Company, for Bob Kechler. They sold fair, and, fact of business, they could have sold better than what they was, because some places you can't get them. The people ask me about them now, but I don't know where to tell them to get them. The only thing that Bob was doing was cutting albums, and he wouldn't cut any singles, and he wouldn't cut but a few of them at a time, you know, and so there never was any royalty statement from him. And so I quit again.

REDD: You've mentioned several times, while we've been talking, Elmo James. Can you tell us a little bit about Elmo James?

CRUDUP: Well, Elmo James was a mighty fine fellow. We used to work together—me and Elmo and Sonny Boy. We played a lot together. We used to live not too far apart in the Mississippi Delta—from '48 up until '50 we lived three quarters of a mile apart. And we used to play together a whole lot.

REDD: Did Elmo James and also Sonny Boy Williamson work
            as radio announcers, that you know of?

CRUDUP: Yeah, Sonny Boy and Elmo used to be over at the King
            Biscuit Company, for a while, and that's the only thing
            I know about it. When I met them, we all were working
            on a farm. Once a week, why, they would go to Belzona,
            and cut a record, you know, a tape for the King Biscuit
            Company. But outside of that I never knew Elmo to be
            a radio announcer.

REDD: With the tremendous knowledge that you have of music,
            having seen it grow from the forties or the thirties into
            what it is today, are there times when you listen to what
            the young kids are playing today and pick out elements
            of artists that you knew in the forties or thirties?

CRUDUP: Yeah, well, you take this young bunch, they love the rock
            and roll. And all of it sprung from the blues. Fact of
            business, there are not very many old blues singers now
            —no, they all are just about dead. You know we lost in
            the last year—one of the best blues singers is gone, and
            that's Fred MacDowell. Do you remember him?

REDD: No, I'm sorry, I don't.

CRUDUP: Yeah, he was a blues singer. One of the old blues singers.
            We all are getting pretty old. I'm just about next to the
            oldest one now that hasn't passed away. Sonny Boy, and
            Elmo—all of those is gone. They was regular blues sing-
            ers.

REDD: What would you say to young people to get them to know
            —I guess I'm speaking more of young black kids—to
            know and appreciate the blues a little better? What can
            you say to our youngsters?

CRUDUP: Well you can't say anything to them to make them real-
            ize, because they feel that if they're not playing a rock,
            that people don't enjoy it. But you take now the white
            people—the white young people are more interested in
            the blues than the young colored people, because they
            begin to see things that they have been missing. They can
            get it now.And the young colored people seem to think
            that if it's not rock, you aren't getting what you want,
            because you take the white teen-ager—he will just go to
            a place, sit on the floor, fill up all the chairs and sit there

and just listen. But the colored kids—if you aren't out dancing, why you are not enjoying yourself. So there isn't anything you can tell them. You just have to let them feel it themselves.

REDD: What does the blues mean to you?

CRUDUP: Well, the blues means to me, you and everyone else—it's a feeling. And the blues are based on just how a person is treated. If you feel mistreated, you got the blues. And if you don't feel mistreated, you don't have no blues. And the more you are mistreated, and the more you think of it, the better the blues sound to you. It's just like a religious song. There are some songs that you can sing— people can be singing and they don't touch you. Then there's one song, you probably run across and sing, you just have a funny feeling; it just goes all over you. Proba- bly makes you feel like you want to cry. And then the other songs—you love them, but you just pass them up. And so that's what the blues is based on—the way a person's feeling.

REDD: Do you see any real difference between what is called blues, rhythm and blues, rock and roll?

CRUDUP: Well, you don't get as much feeling out of rock and roll and rhythm as you do out of blues. You take the blues —it means more than some people understand. A col- ored person ought to realize what the blues is because he's been having the blues all his life. He was born in the blues, which I was. I don't know whether you were, but I was. My mother and father weren't married. My daddy gave me four dollars and a pocket knife from the time I was born in the world up until this day. And I couldn't get things like other kids because I had nobody to take care of me but my mother. And wages were cheap. And, then, fact of business, during the whole time that she was carrying me, she had the blues, because her and my daddy weren't married and didn't marry. And so there you are—there's nothing but the blues for you. And then you worked on jobs with white people and they pay you this, and pay him that, and it takes just as much for you to live as it does him, but yet and still, there you are. I'm concerned with the blues. That's why mostly I started to sing the blues, was this: I worked, and when the end of the season come, I had just as much when the end as as I did when I started. I made many a day for fifty cents I don't mean fifty cents an hour—fifty cents a day. And had a wife and one kid to take care of. And part of the time the man'd pay me and part of the time, he wouldn't. See? Then I worked my family on a farm, and the man would tell me, to my face that if the plantation had come out of debt, I would've cleared seventeen hundred dollars. And nobody on the plantation cleared a dollar—the plantation come out in debt, and we didn't get anything. And that was a whole year's work for just something to eat. And so, if that don't give you the blues, there ain't no way in the world for you ever to have the blues.

REDD: Where do you think the music that you've spent much of your life playing and developing—where is this music headed now?

CRUDUP: Well, it's headed to the top. Not too long ago I was asked, "Do you reckon would the blues ever go out of existence?" No, not as long as the world stands. Course, all that older bunch is dying out, but it's still in the South: some teen-agers coming up that is loving the blues and think that blues is the only way to go and they'll be on up directly. And so, now you take—it's more white kids, playing the blues than you ever heard in your life. It's been all the time, that if you couldn't play sentimental music, and all of that, you couldn't play for white people. But now, they don't want to hear that stuff. They just want to hear the blues. I was out in California, and there were some white people came from Texas to California to hear me and to see me, so they told me.

REDD: You mention having gotten some of your training in the church. Do you see a relationship between music in the church and the blues? All the same? Different? What?

CRUDUP: Well, the blues and the music in the church is all on the same base. It's no different. You cut some notes in the church and you leave them for the blues. That's the only difference. But if you started playing a church song and nobody sang it, and you started playing the blues and nobody sang it, you couldn't tell it apart.

REDD: Have you played black colleges or black universities?

CRUDUP: No, no, I tell you now, no. I played all—for the last five years I've been playing colleges and universities and blues tours, and it's all been white colleges. I haven't played no colored colleges.

REDD: Are there other blues singers that you know that have been taken advantage of by people like Lester Melrose?

CRUDUP: All I know of. All I know have had the same trouble I've had. And there's Fred MacDowell—he's dead now—he's got many a many dollar hung up and didn't get it. And I've got many a one hung up, and they claim to be trying to get it for me. I may be able to see it and I may not. And so, you know how it is with people . . . Some of them —they don't want to sue, then you turn around and you switch the thing and if it was you or I, they'd get it. But, it's just turned around, why? And if they get it, why? And so, I'm supposed to get some money from these records. But now, when, I couldn't tell you.

Jerry Butler

One of the all-time great classics in the music world is the 1958 recording of "Your Precious Love" by the Impressions and Jerry Butler. Despite their joint success in the fifties, Jerry Butler left the Impressions in 1960 to perform as a single artist. He received accep- tance with "He Will Break Your Heart," "When Trouble Calls," and "Isle of Siren." He achieved success with "Make It Easy on Your- self," one of the early Hal David and Bert Bachrach songs. Another little-known fact outside of black America is that Jerry Butler was the first artist to record the Henry Mancini classic, "Moon River," which outsold all later versions.

As a songwriter, Jerry Butler has written or been the coauthor of some of America's finest music, including "I've Been Lovin' You Too Long," "Brand New Me," "Never Gonna Give You Up," and "Western Union Man."

He heads his own music publishing company, Fountain Produc- tions, based in Chicago, and is deeply involved in guiding and pro- tecting the talents of future young writers. Among black performers, he represents the new awareness. In addition to being superbly talented, he is knowledgeable about his business. His basic philosophy of viewing show business as two words, "show" and "business," is the direction in which the new black artist is moving.

Throughout the recording industry, Butler is respected as a true gentleman, affectionately referred to as the "Ice Man" by his admirers because of his smooth manner of performing on stage. He is well aware of the impact mass media can have upon our music.

The following interview with Jerry Butler took place in the offices of his publishing company in Chicago in August 1971.

REDD: Jerry, I have seen For Whatever's Fair—is that a joint production company between you and Gene Chandler?

BUTLER: No, actually it is owned by Gene, but since For Whatever's Fair was born at the time of the Gene and Jerry Album, we decided to use "Whatever's Fair" to help get For Whatever's Fair established. Actually, the album was produced by him and myself, so consequently everybody just assumed that For Whatever's Fair was a joint venture, but that was the only thing we did as a joint venture under that particular title, you know.

REDD: How long have you been writing songs?

BUTLER: Well, since high school—I was with a group called the Quails, which we started in high school. We just ran out of birds, so we started using partridges and all kinds of fowl, you know, as names. I had written a song called "If Love Is Wrong," and my father passed just about that time. So I had to assume the lead, being the oldest boy and all that, and I had to give up the singing idea altogether and go to work. Between work and school, it just didn't leave a whole lot of time for the other thing, so the fellows kept the group together. When they recorded a song and somehow they forgot that I had written it, and somebody else got credit as the writer and it went through a whole thing. But out of that came my introduction to the Impressions, who were at that time called the Roosters, a bunch of cats from Chattanooga, Tennessee—Arthur Brooks, Richard Brooks, and Sam Gooden. They did some things near one of the guys in that original group of the Quails that I was involved with. And when they came here I was in my last year, my senior year, of high school. They were trying to find a person to take the place of two of the guys in their group who had not come from Chattanooga with them, and I was called to act as a replacement until they could find somebody on a permanent basis. So I was kind of a replacement for the guys who didn't come from down there; in turn, I brought Curtis Mayfield into the group. Then we sat down and composed "For Your Precious Love"—Arthur, Richard Brooks, and myself. And that was the kind of thing that launched our career per se. But even in school I was always writing poetry and that whole kind of thing. And the reason I mention that is because now that I am actually publishing music and this kind of thing I get a lot of poems from young kids who want to be songwriters and I try to explain to them that a poem is a poem, anything without music is a poem, you see. So they send me, a lot of times on notebook paper, what have you, beautiful poems, and they say, "Will you put it to music?" That's very difficult to do because songs are not written that way, you know,—The song and the melody and the rhythm and all of that have to come together almost at the same time if it is going to be a great song. Now there are some exceptions to that rule, however, like "The Twelfth of Never" was basically a riddle song. You know the riddle song is like "I gave my love a cherry that had no stone; I gave my love a chicken that had no bone," you know that kind of thing. Then they took that particular melody and changed the words and entitled it "The Twelfth of Never."

REDD: Of all the songs that you have written, which are your favorite selections?

BUTLER: Baldwin once said that my next book is the best book. You know, I kind of like to think that it's the next song that I write. A song with me is like a brand-new love affair, it's like all brand new and exciting, and you always figure that this is going to be the best one ever, you know.

REDD: What have been some of the ones that have done well for you?

BUTLER: Oh, well . . .

REDD: That you've written, or been a coauthor of.

BUTLER: Let's see—"For Your Precious Love," of course, "He Will Break Your Heart," "A Brand New Me," "I Stand Accused," "I've Been Lovin' You Too Long," "Western Union Man," "Never Gonna Give You Up."

REDD: You mentioned "I've Been Lovin' You Too Long." You wrote that with the late Otis Redding.

BUTLER: Yes. And that was one of the little fun experiences that happen to people, I guess, in their life. Because we were scattered so far apart, it was really kind of funny the way it all worked out. What happened was there was a young boy here in Chicago that brought me on an acetate the thing "I've Been Lovin' You Too Long." And that was all that was on it. And he said, "Jerry, I don't know if there's a song in it or not but if you can I wish you would finish it"; so I took the idea and started hassling with it. And I was flying to Atlanta and I finished maybe the first two verses of it, so when I got to Atlanta I was in a first class. They've got a little first class lounge there. And I was sitting in there, and Otis popped in, and we started laughing and talking about some things and found that he and I were both going to Buffalo, New York, the very next day and had no idea that we were going to be on the very same show. So we wound up there in the town and we played a place called the Music Hall, and that night back in the hotel we got a bottle and we sat around banging on the guitar. He was showing me some tunes that he had written and never been able to finish, and so out of the conversation I said, "Well, here's a thing that I've been working on man for six months, let's say, and I can't get past the second verse to save my life, you know." So he listened and picked out the chord changes on it and said, "Hey, man, that's a smash!" I said, "Well if it's a smash you do it and when you finish, whatever happens, I'll split the writing and publishing and every-thing with you, right?" So he said "O.K., I'm going to do that," and we laughed, you know. How many times have you known a cat to say, "I'm going to do that," man, and you never hear from him again. Anyway I went to De-troit after that. He called me in Detroit and said, "I've recorded that tune, man, and it's a smash." I said, "Yeh, I know it's a smash, man. It ain't even on the streets yet, and you talk about it's a smash." He said, "Naw Jerry, this is a smash." And I said, "O.K., fine." Went to Atlanta and heard it on the radio, you know, and I said, "Gee that song sounds familiar." And I went over to a friend's house, and he said "Hey listen, man, you've got the new Otis Redding thing; it's a smash." So he's playing it for me and I said, "Yeh I'm hip to that song. I wrote it." But the beautiful part of it was that I think that seventy percent of the success of "I've Been Lovin' You Too Long" was the way that Otis did it and not necessarily the song itself. Otis just cried and died and moaned and groaned all through that thing. You know, it was just his thing because at the time I needed a hit badder than anybody, you know, and for me to give away a hit song was just ridiculous. But I think the way he did it was really what made it happen.

REDD: Now you worked with Otis, who was really a great songwriter; but you also worked with Gamble and Huff and also Curtis Mayfield.

BUTLER: "He Will Break Your Heart" with Curtis Mayfield. You know, when I pick a partner I pick the best partners ever. I just get all the heavies, you know, to come in and all sorts.

REDD: There are so many songwriters that are never known. Can we get into some of those people?

BUTLER: Yeh sure, well, I can think of the guy who's partly responsible for Elvis Presley's successes was a black fellow from New York, known as Otis Blackwell. A lot of people used to see his name on records and never knew that he was black or anything about him, you see, because they never did for Otis Blackwell what they did for Jim Webb, let us say. You know, Jim Webb would write a song, and before you knew it everywhere you looked someone was recording a Jim Webb tune. Otis Blackwell wrote four or five million sellers for Elvis Presley, and nobody ever even saw his face. Fellow by the name of Titus Turner in collaboration with some other fellows wrote a song called "Fever." The whole copyright and everything, I think, was sold for about fifty dollars or some crazy stuff like that. You know it just goes on and on. L. C. Cook, Sam Cook's brother, who was responsible for most of Sam Cook's songs that were very big. And I know that there are a whole bunch of others. Percy Mayfield, who was a blues singer in his own right but composed a lot of things for Ray Charles, such as "Hit the Road Jack" and some other things. And then there was Louie Jordan, who was one of the greatest of all time songwriters but no one ever knew that. They just knew him as a saxophonist and a singer. Nat Cole, you know.

REDD: Why do you think, Jerry, that we just don't know about black songwriters?

BUTLER: Guys like W. C. Handy, and all the old black writers after they passed on or whatever, you know, then they started to get some kind of publicity because some white artist or some black superstar decided to do their works. But basically, with the contemporary artists that was a whole thing first of all that they were the nontalents, you see, that they were basically writing in very hip form with hip meaning. What is happening today would not have any bearing on what may be happening ten, fifteen, twenty years from now. And the whole thing has been, I feel, that nobody has ever really taken those songs for what they're really worth, and just explored the talent or publicized the talent of that particular writer. I can think of a Curtis Mayfield. Now you know that everybody writes about Bob Dylan being the great folk writer and that whole kind of thing. Very few issues speak of Curtis Mayfield as a writer, you know, and Curtis has been writing about the times long before the times were happening. You know, he was writing about things like "We're a Winner," "Keep on Pushing," "Choice of Colors," "This Is My Country," you know, things that were so relevant to the times. "This Is My Country," as a matter of fact, if it had been written by a white writer would have been played on the big pop stations, but because it was written by a black writer, sung by a black group, see, a lot of big 50,000-watt stations' program directors sitting on top of those stations say, "Well, this is a little inflammatory in content, you know, and I just can't dig a fellow saying, 'And folks, some people say we ain't got the right to say that this is my country. Before they give in, they'd rather fuss and fight than say this is my country.' " I can't see anything inflammatory in that, you know, but then I'm not programing those particular stations, and I think that's one of the reasons for it. We are always at the mercy of white critics, white program directors, white whatever, you see. So until we become black critics, black program directors, and can speak to our music as we hear it and as we feel it and speak what we know about, you know, then it's always going to be subdued and of less importance in the whole general scheme of things than the pop or the white counterpart of our music. I played a concert in Washington, D.C., and the critics just panned it to pieces. You know they said that the "Ice Man" was very, very cool—matter of fact was so cool that a lot of people didn't really groove with what he was doin'. Now, the next day I called up the writer, the cat that wrote the article, and invited him for lunch. So he came by, and the first thing out of his mouth was apologetic. He said, "Man, I'm not really a critic, you know. Plus classical music is my thing, you know." And so forth and so on, and "I had to do it because the papers signed me to do it. Right? So I just wrote about it, and you know the way I felt about it." Here's a cat that never even listens to a Jerry Butler per se, you know. He thought the Edwin Hawkins singers were too frantic, and they were on the billing with me, and a whole bunch of things that he couldn't even relate to. Yet he was writing about it in the mass media, you know, and signing his name to it. And a lot of people were going to like or dislike what I do based on what he said. And he didn't know a damn thing about it.

REDD: Jerry, what are you doing now? What's going on? I know you're involved in different things, but what's taking place now, and what guarantee is there that these times are going to be corrected?

BUTLER: Well, last year in October the Reverend Jesse Jackson came up with the idea for an institution called the Institution of Black American Music, and I got involved with it, and we got the thing incorporated. We're going to start moving on that this year and that is going to speak directly to the amount of publicity given to black music in all its forms. Not just rhythm and blues per se but jazz and gospel and the blues and whatever black folks are doing in music. You know we're going to make a record of that. We're going to contact all of the memorable experiences in that, I mean you take Leadbelly, for instance, the guy who wrote "Irene, Good Night," which is a big country and western tune, and I would venture to say that ninety percent of all the black people in America don't even know that Leadbelly wrote it or that Leadbelly was black, for that matter! Things like that come to mind that all of the great blues singers like Ma Rainey and folks of that nature who have long since died, and there are tapes and records and even some video things on these particular people that have not been collected by any black group. I mean we don't have 'em. They have 'em in the archives in Washington, D.C., or they may have it in the Columbia Record Library or whatever. But we should have that, we should control that. I mean that is ours, you know. So we should know where those things are and we should have them and we should be able to open it up so black school children can come in and see what blacks have contributed to the music. I mean there have been some fantastic works by black composers in classical fields and in other media that nobody even knows about, you know, black or white for that matter, because it just hasn't been spoken to on that kind of basis. This is what the institution is all about, to collect all the things past and to bring folks up to date on that and to capture what is happening now and what will be happening in the future and to have a continuous flow of black talent and the music that they contributed to and even to the point that we are going to develop critics who are going to speak to the music as it were, as honestly as possible.

REDD: Our music is not taught in the public school system. What can educators do to complement the effort that is now taking place?

BUTLER: Well, that is a very good question. See for years I found
          that basically, your black educational institutions were
          the most hypocritical in the outlook of music. I remember
          when Howard University would not have even a black
          jazz artist at Howard University. They would bring in
          some white group to hold the seminars and this kind of
          thing. And that was based on the people who ran the
          school; they just had less regard for Cannonball Adderly.
          They would have classical music rather than the blues. In
          the meantime Yale and Harvard were buying John Lee
          Hooker and Lenny Wallace, you know, and we were
          studying Mendelssohn and Wagner and those folks, you
          see. So it was that kind of thing that's been happening.
          Now, I'm thankful to say it's not happening any more.
          I played a white college long before I ever played a black
          college, you know. So that speaks to a whole kind of
          thing, and I think basically it all came about because
          people who had gone to college and had been exposed to
          Brahms, Beethoven, and Bach wanted basically to forget
          about the blues because to them the blues was a part of
          the thing that they wanted to escape from rather than
          being part of the life style, you see. So now that we have
          become more aware of who we are and what the blues
          are all about and how it relates to black people in general,
          we are starting to deal with that. Now as a real instance,
          like B. B. King has been rediscovered by white folks so
          all of a sudden now B. B. King is being heard again on
          black stations. Well, it's my feeling that B. B. King never
          should have stopped being heard on black stations.

REDD: Jerry, you are one of America's great songwriters. What
          has been the relationship between the publishing compa-
          nies and the songwriters over the years?

BUTLER: Well, for the most part the songwriter-publisher relation-
          ship is a partnership. Whereas the publisher says to the
          writer, "I will take your work and publicize it, cause it
          to be recorded, make sure that there is sheet music avail-
          able throughout the country, and collect the money for
          you, handle all the administration and everything. For
          that I will receive fifty percent of all the money that's
          brought in and the rest of the other fifty percent will go
          directly to you." In rhythm and blues, or in jazz per se,

most of the time the writers or the person who created
the music were also performing the music. So that eliminated the publisher's having that particular work recorded because the composer had already recorded it.
And this is why a lot of blacks started opening their own
publishing companies. Say for myself, most of the things
that I've written I have recorded and they've been hits.
So I really did not need a publisher to see that I got the
particular work recorded. What I did need a publisher
for, however, was to make sure that I was getting all of
the monies that were due to me from the record companies and the performing societies, that whole administra-
tion situation, which is more important after the fact than
anything else to a writer. See, there is a relationship
between not only what happens on a national level, but
what happens to your material on an international level.
In fact, Curtis Mayfield just recently returned from
Europe and found out that some of the old things they
had recorded with the Impressions are just starting to be
exposed and become big, you know, throughout England
and France and some of those places. So the one thing I
would like to say to young folks who are going to be
starting publishing companies and that sort of thing, is
that it is great to have your own publishing company, but
there is so much about publishing that you need to know,
that maybe for the first two or three years, you see, you
should make an alliance with a white firm or some sort
to get that knowledge and that expertise to learn how to
deal with the performance societies and the international
societies so that you realize every penny that you have
coming to you as a publisher and as a writer.

REDD: What is the highest compliment that you could pay the
             black writer as he is to today's popular music?

BUTLER: The writer is basically the foundation of the popular
             music scene. And being that the foundation is the most
             important part of any structure—I think that's the high-
             est compliment that I could pay to a writer. You see, a
             great talent is a great talent, but without a great vehicle
             he is just a great talent doing a lesser work. If you get a
             great work for a talent to perform, you usually have a

great record, which usually creates a lot of other great things. But I think basically it all starts with the man's idea and his pen and the fact that he can put this on a piece of paper and disseminate the idea so as to show it to a whole bunch of great talents. And he is definitely the foundation of the record industry. Without the writer, I mean, we don't really have anything to deal with.

REDD: Are there some things that you would like to say personally, things that you have seen over the years that you have a message to youngsters, to Americans?

BUTLER: You know, the Boy Scout motto to me has always been a very hip motto, you know, whether it's relating to the Boy Scouts or to the movement in the nation or whatever. To be prepared is very important, dig. And like when you take into consideration what preparedness means, uh, the songwriter per se, myself, I don't play any instruments, write any music, so whenever I do anything I am at a handicap. So it would be my suggestion to anybody that wants to get into the musical thing, to learn as much about this industry as he would to be a doctor or a lawyer or anything else. See, there are the Volkswagons of this industry and the Rolls Royces of this industry, the VW being just equipped to do basic transportation as the Rolls Royce is a kind of a luxury thing and has everything. So in instance of a Donny Hathaway who is a Rolls Royce type, you know—I mean Donny can write, can arrange, can do anything he wants to do because he not only has the talent, he has the academic knowledge to put with that talent. He was born with the soul, so that ain't no problem. He was born with the talent, so that ain't no problem. All the rest of it he had to go out and get, you see, but all of that comes from that preparedness thing. So every young person aspiring to become anything in this music industry should not only know how much soul he has, how much talent he has, but should follow to the fullest extent his ability to learn. Not only learn about music itself, but about business, because we deal with this as show business. We try to make one word of this, but it's two words. It's *show*, which is what happens on stage and what happens on camera and what happens; but *business* is what happens after you come off that stage and after the cameras stop rolling and you start dealing with pennies and dollars and hundreds of thousands of dollars and millions of dollars. To be able to deal with that is what we have to know about, and I think it's been one of the big hangups and the reason black music hasn't moved farther than it has is because most of the giants have not been able to deal with anything other than the show, you see. So that's the big problem.

REDD: One final question. Gamble, Huff, and Butler have changed the course of music in this country. I can't say any more than that, but I'd like for you to comment on it.

BUTLER: Gamble and Huff and myself got involved just over short periods of time, but we were fortunate in that we all felt the music the same way, and we were able to express ourselves to each other in such a fashion that the product that we made was well liked throughout the country and probably throughout the world. There are many places it's been heard. You know, I think it was a great experience for me and I think they feel the same way about it.

Jessie Whitaker

Shortly after World War II my grandparents, Andrew and Ida Bell Redd moved from Arkansas into the southeastern Missouri hamlet of Hermandale, about ten miles north of Blythville, Arkansas. Among their new neighbors were Mr. and Mrs. John James, the parents of Jessie Whitaker, baritone singer with the famous Pilgrim Travelers gospel quartet.

Beginning in 1947 the Pilgrim Travelers became a legend in black America, recording such songs as "Peace of Mind," "It Is No Secret," "Shake My Mother's Hand," and "After Awhile." They made gospel classics out of "Straight Street," "Look to the Hills," "I've Got a New Home," and "How Jesus Died." The last two songs were written by Jessie Whitaker. And "How Jesus Died" was changed into "Lonely Avenue" by Doc Pomus and remains one of Ray Charles' greatest all-time hit recordings.

In his book *The Gospel Sound,* Tony Heilbut writes of the Pilgrim Travelers: "The strongest harmonic asset was their baritone, Jessie Whitaker, who had the most beautiful quartet baritone I've ever heard. A fine insiduously seductive vocalist up front, Whitaker produced unique harmonic effects with his voice."*

The gospel group was comprised of other well-known singers, including at one time the famous Lou Rawls. By the time the Pilgrim Travelers decided to disband in the late 1950s, they had already secured their place in gospel history. Later, Whitaker returned to his home in Hermandale and joined a gospel group called the Silver Bells.

Through my cousin, William Edmondson, I arranged to interview the noted singer. Late one evening in July 1972 I pulled my car into the yard of Mr. and Mrs. John James, and finally met and spoke with Jessie Whitaker, baritone of the legendary Pilgrim Travelers.

REDD: Mr. Whitaker, if I were to ask who is Jessie Whitaker, a member of the Pilgrim Travelers, how would you define that?

WHITAKER: Well, I would say, I was raised where I was born, raised in the country, right here in southeast Missouri. And I started out singing right here. So, I left here and went to St. Louis. I joined a group and sang a little bit; then I left there and went to Chicago, and I joined the Kansas City Gospel Singers, out of Kansas City, Missouri. And I went to California, met the Pilgrim Travelers, and that's when I started with them.

REDD: Who were members of the Pilgrim Travelers when you met them in Los Angeles?

WHITAKER: There was J.W. Alexander, singing tenor and manager; there was Keith Barber, singing lead; Kylo Turner, singing lead; Rafael Taylor, singing bass; and there was another young man singing baritone just before I joined them. He quit—his name was Robinson—and I took his place.

REDD: Is there an interesting story about how you came to meet the Pilgrim Travelers?

WHITAKER: Well, yes, there is. I was in Oakland, California, at the

*Tony Heilbut, *The Gospel Sound* (New York: Simon and Schuster, 1971), p. 115.

time, singing with a group called the Golden Harps, with Paul Foster. I sang with Paul Foster before he joined the Soul Stirrers. We had a group there in Oakland. So we were singing there. And so the Pilgrim Travelers heard that I was in California, and they called from New York City, and asked would I join them when they got back? And I told them I would think about it. So when they got there, I thought about it, and I said, "Well, maybe I'll go on this tour with you." And I went on that tour with them and I liked it. And we came back and got a contract with Speciality and we started recording. And I stayed with them.

REDD: So you actually were with the Pilgrim Travelers when the first record with Speciality was made?

WHITAKER: That's right, I was.

REDD: What was the first record you recorded with Specialty, if you remember, and what year, if you can recall?

WHITAKER: Oh, let's see. That would be back in 1947. Now the numbers, I can't recall right now. But I can tell you, two of our hit numbers was "Mother Bowed" and "Jesus Met the Woman at the Well." That was the numbers that really went over—that sold.

REDD: What was the fellow's name that wrote "Mother Bowed"?

WHITAKER: That was L.C. Henry, out of Detroit.

REDD: What were the tours like? You mentioned that you were on tour and the Pilgrim Travelers were on tour, and I recall my cousin, William Edmondson, really drilling into my head very graphically some of the performances that you and the Pilgrim Travelers would do when you would come through Hermandale when I went to high school, but it seemed like it was one of the most exciting kinds of cultural baptisms that I've always missed, you know. And I've tried to capture it a little bit but I just don't think I've ever been able to describe just what that whole circuit of gospel entertainment was like. Can you tell us what it was like?

WHITAKER: Well, I would say it was real beautiful. And I enjoyed every moment of it. Really, you have to know Jesus to really get into this type of singing. You can't just get up there and just sing. You've got to have a feeling to do it. And I've always had that feeling, ever since I was a real young man. I got religion right here, baptized here, and I started out singing here. And I really enjoyed it, and we had some wonderful times together.

REDD: What are some of the other Pilgrim Travelers doing now? Do you ever keep in touch with them?

WHITAKER: Oh, yes, There's Kylo Turner, one of our main lead singers, was very popular throughout this country. Now he's in Chicago. He's singing there now with a group. And I have a group here now that I'm singing with, called Silver Bells, and we are booking them up in Portersville, and I'm hoping to see him. Now, Alexander, the manager and tenor singer, he's in Beverly Hills, California, and he's doing very well. He's got his own office; he's writing music, and he's doing great.

REDD: That's beautiful, that's beautiful. You wrote some very famous songs. Any particular favorites of yours?

WHITAKER: Yes. "How Jesus Died." I wrote that one, and that was in Charlotte, North Carolina. We were on a program that night, and we got back to the hotel, and for some reason, I couldn't go to sleep. It looked like this song was in my mind. So I just got up—it just happened there was a Bible there in the hotel—so I started reading the Bible, and George McCurn, our bass singer, I woke him up. And we started reading the Bible, and started picking out words, and that's how I wrote that.

REDD: How did you feel later on when Ray Charles came out with a song—Ray Charles didn't write it; I think a fellow by the name of Doc Pomus wrote it—but was called "Lonely Avenue," and it sounded just like "How Jesus Died." How did that make you feel?

WHITAKER: Well, it wasn't quite like "Jesus Died," but in between another number that I wrote like "I've Got a New Home." It's kind of in between. The only thing I regret is that I didn't make the money off of "New Home" that he made off that one. That's the only thing. I knew Ray Charles very well. We were very good friends. And we enjoyed talking to each other, and we'd get ideas from each other whenever we'd meet.

REDD: What would you say the Pilgrim Travelers are most famous for? What particular thing would you say the Pilgrim Travelers did during their existence?

WHITAKER: Well, there's a couple of things. I would say that we were, according to the people, we usually were the best-dressed group, and we had the best record of singing, according to the people. We were the best, at the time.

REDD: I've always heard the very same thing. Right now, I would say that there is really no organized visual documentation of black music anywhere. Yet the Pilgrim Travelers were regular guests on television. Can you give us a little background on some of the things you did on television?

WHITAKER: Well, in Los Angeles, we did quite a bit of television work. Down at City Hall, they called us the "Good Will Workers." And I can't recall the guy that we did do television for. But he was a swell guy—he was a white guy. And any time we were in town, we would be on his program. He was a very great guy. And we did quite a bit of work. And down in West Virginia, we did a little television work. So, I think we did very good on it.

REDD: If my memory serves me right, I recall that Ed Sullivan booked the Pilgrim Travelers several times.

WHITAKER: Well, we never did really get on the Ed Sullivan Show. Because, at the time that he was ready for us, that was the time that we were just about breaking up. We were just in the prime to really get going. But some of the fellows after some of the old guys quit, like Turner—he quit—then there's Barber—he quit. Then we had to reorganize, and we picked up Lou Rawls, and we picked up another fellow called Booker, which was great. They were great. And we were on our way really again. But then they decided to do something else. So —you see where Lou Rawls is at; and the little fellow,

Booker, he's pastor—he's got a big church there in
Fort Worth, Texas. He's doing beautifully.

REDD: Was there some particular reason that caused the Pilgrim Travelers to finally disperse as a group? I seem to recall that Lou Rawls mentioned once that there was an automobile accident that he was in, or the Pilgrim Travelers were in, which kind of put things at bay for a while, and it was difficult during those particular times. Do you recall anything similar to that?

WHITAKER: That's right, yes, uh huh. In 1950, the Pilgrim Travelers had a wreck. We had a head-on collision near Hot Springs, California. Not Hot Springs—Palm Springs, California, and we were laid up for a month or so. So, that hurt. That hurt us pretty bad. One of the fellows got his vocal cords—Barber, to be exact, Keith Barber —he got his vocal cords messed up a little. And he couldn't sing for a year. He could sing, but he couldn't raise his voice—he could sing on a level. So that hurt us. And as the years go on, I guess the guys got disgusted or something. Then one left; then another one left; then we got Lou. Then after Sam Cooke went off in the pop field, he did very well; and Lou Rawls decided he would try it. And so that kind of split the group up. The group—we could have gone into pop, but that just wasn't my style. That just wasn't me. I didn't like that. I just didn't go for it. So, that was the end of the group.

REDD: Recently, there has been a resurgence in gospel music. I brought two albums down with me from the radio station: The Pilgrim Travelers' "Shake My Mother's Hand" and "The Best of the Pilgrim Travelers Volume Number 2" and so there must be a Volume Number 1.

WHITAKER: Now, there's another Pilgrim Travelers. After the old group dispersed, I organized another group. And they are still singing. I was with them last Sunday night in St. Louis.

REDD: Is that right?

WHITAKER: Right. And we had a very wonderful time. And they're doing recording and they're very good.

REDD: Well, that's really beautiful to hear. Was that a formal appearance with the Pilgrim Travelers that you made?

WHITAKER: Yes. They were having a program up there in which they were giving away a queen-size bedroom set, and they called me about two weeks in advance and asked me would I come? And I told them I would. They didn't take chances on me coming up there. They came down and picked me up, and drove me back to St. Louis.

REDD: Is there a great deal of difference between how gospel groups perform today and how gospel groups performed back in the forties during the time that perhaps gospel music, quartet music, was most prominent?

WHITAKER: Oh, yes, there's a lot of difference. The groups now sing much different from what we were singing then. Most of them sing much louder, they sing much faster, and all of them got—some of them got just too much music, that's all, for gospel singing, I think. They got drum, they got bass guitar, they got regular guitar. And it's just too much for gospel singing, I believe.

REDD: You mentioned that there was too much music. Now, did you often sing a cappella, or you know, did you use a guitar, or just how much music did you use?

WHITAKER: Back then, we didn't use any music. We were doing it all a cappella. We really didn't have to have any music. And what was so nice about it then, if you sang a cappella, you could always know when someone made a mistake. You could hear. And that would make the groups really be careful and really sing. Now, it doesn't matter. You can get in and make a mistake all you want to, but the music covers it up. And that's what happens. Most of the guitar players, they play louder than the singers are singing. You can only hear the lead singer—no background. And see, I love the harmony—that's what I really loved. And nowadays, they don't have much of it. If they do, you can't hear it.

REDD: Listening to the Temptations, I personally find that the Temptations' background is strikingly similar to

that of the Pilgrim Travelers. How would you charac-
terize my observation there?

WHITAKER: You're right. I listen to them quite a bit. When I was
in Los Angeles, I listened to those fellows all the time.
I think they sing beautifully. And you're right, what
you're saying.

REDD: Who are some of the persons in gospel music that
you've enjoyed association with that you think have
also made important contributions to black music in
America?

WHITAKER: I would say the Soul Stirrers out of Chicago, and both
blind groups: The Five Blind Boys out of Mississippi
and also Alabama, and the Dixie Hummingbirds. We
were some of the first groups to come along, and we
traveled together quite a bit, you know. And there's
a group down in Memphis that came along a little
later and did a very good job, which is the Spirit of
Memphis.

REDD: In terms of movement, I've always characterized and
whenever I lecture to high school classes I've tried to
tell them that the movements that guys like the Temptations or the Impressions or some of the other groups
get into are actually taken from gospel music. Can you
give me a little bit of background on that—how those
movements came about and just a little history on
that?

WHITAKER: Well, that's true. That's why most of your rock and
roll and that kind of music—they got that movement
from gospel singing and they got it from the gospel
groups. And some of them, I would say, they make the
move just to be doing it. And some of them really had
the feeling to do it. You really have to have a feeling.
You have to have that intimate spirit, you know, telling you what to do, and how to do it. And when you
get started, there's nothing you can do about it—you
do it. And that's the way it came about.

REDD: Now, when you are singing and you are really involved in the music and really feeling what you're
singing, what is going through your mind during that
particular time? On records here, it's quite different

than the live performance. The live performance may
just go on and on and on. And today, when a gospel
group do an improvised kind of ending on a song, it's
really taken from gospel music. What did you do to
carry it on and to end it? How did you know when to
end and how far to carry it on?

WHITAKER: Well, it's hard to say. When you get started singing
and start feeling good, usually someone has to set you
down, you know. You can't really stop it yourself. It's
just that feeling—you get going and you just can't
stop. So that's what happens.

REDD: There was a song that the Pilgrim Travelers did called
"Move Off of Broadway onto Straight Street." It's one
of the most dramatic songs to perform, you know, that
I recall, How did that particular song come about?

WHITAKER: That's my arrangement. That's not my words, but
that's my arrangement. I happened to find that in a
songbook, and arranged it that way. I just happened
to be looking through the book and I saw the words
and I liked them. So I called the guys together and say,
"How do you like this? It'd go this way." So, that's
what happened. I arranged that myself.

REDD: What is the significance of "Move Off of Broadway
onto Straight Street"?

WHITAKER: Well, that means when you are living in sin, and
you're doing a little of everything that you shouldn't
do, it's really—to bring it down to a natural fact—it's
really when you're doing wrong and you decide to do
right. That's all to it.

REDD: Another song that you wrote was "I've Got a New
Home." How about that one?

WHITAKER: Oh, yes. I picked that song out of a couple of two or
three different songs, oh, way back, long years ago, so
I just happened to hear a few words from other
groups, and I took a word from that group, and then
added my own words to it, and that's how "New
Home" came about.

REDD: What are some of the others that you recall that you
wrote for the group?

WHITAKER: Well, I'm trying to remember now. There's another

one "I Can Do Better Than That." Remember that?
Well, it's from a story like Samson, you know, how
strong he was. Then he got weak and let a woman get
to him, you know. So that's how that come about. I
figured that happened to him, well, I figure I could do
better than that.

REDD: What was the reception that the Pilgrim Travelers
would get when they traveled from town to town?
How did we treat the Pilgrim Travelers?

WHITAKER: Oh, beautifully. We had a wonderful time just about
every place we've gone. We had no trouble no time.
Oh, yeah, sometimes the program would be very lean,
but other times, we'd make it up in another place. We
never had any problems.

REDD: What were the best parts of the country for you to
perform? Any particular section or cities that you
were received better than other places?

WHITAKER: Well, starting in the South. There were a few cities
were just great, like say, Birmingham, Alabama, Atlanta, Georgia, Mobile, Alabama, and New Orleans,
Louisiana, and Houston, Texas. Those was wonderful
cities. We'd never fail in those towns. And coming on
up North: St. Louis was great; Chicago was greater;
Detroit was beautiful; and also Cleveland, Ohio, was
nice. So we had beautiful times in most of those.

REDD: Are there any of the guys out there singing now that
you find that give due credit to some of the forerun-
ners of the music?

WHITAKER: Yes. Just like in St. Louis, last weekend. I met so many
different friends—old-timers, you know—they just
come out especially to hear me sing. They hadn't
heard me in a long time, and the fellows up there told
them that I would be there, and boy—they were there.

REDD: What are some of the songs that you led for the Pilgrim Travelers?

WHITAKER: First thing that I did was "Straight Street," and they
really ate it up. And then "I've Got a New Home."
And that wrapped it up. That was the program!

REDD: Gospel singers have for a long time used the double
lead singers. Pop groups are just getting around to

doing that kind of thing. Did the Pilgrim Travelers
have anything to do with making that a tradition with
gospel groups?

WHITAKER: Well, I want to give credit where credit's due. I would
say the Soul Stirrers started that, a long time ago. The
Soul Stirrers really started it. But when I joined the
Pilgrim Travelers, well, we really had three lead singers. A little guy called Washington—Wintford Washington. He didn't stay with the group very long, but
he was there. So I would say the Soul Stirrers really
started that double lead.

REDD: What about the bass singers? The bass singers are
always very much noted in gospel music. Anybody in
particular that you have come across in your travels
that you would rate as one of the finer bass singers?

WHITAKER: Yes, there's quite a few great bass singers that's been
through the country and was around during the time
I was out there. Now you take—I'll start out with
Jessie Farley of the Soul Stirrers. He was no "Show
me" basser, but he was perfect, and he had a beautiful, smooth bass voice, and he was great. Now when
you come out to the "Show me" basses, I would say
Jimmie Jones, who used to be with the Richmond
Harmonizers—now he was great. And in later years,
there was a guy named George McCurn. We got him
later. He was great—what you call "Show me" gospel basses. He could tear a house down just like a
lead singer could, you know. And that's what you
call a "Show me" bass. So you had quite a few great
basses.

REDD: You use the term "tear the house down." Give me a
description of that.

WHITAKER: That means that shouting, just about everybody in the
church—in the auditorium. That's what it means.

REDD: What kind of feeling could you recall when those
vibrations started to happen?

WHITAKER: Well, then you get happy yourself. You get happy
before they do. And you know when you get that
feeling, they're going to get it, too. If you're meaning
well, they'll get it. And that's it.

REDD: Did the Pilgrim Travelers practice routines? What
             kind of things did you do to prepare yourselves for
             your performances?

WHITAKER: Oh, we kept very busy in rehearsal. We'd rehearse
             most of the time. Whenever we weren't really just
             exhausted, we'd always call the group together and sit
             down in rehearsal and have a little prayer and that was
             our routine.

REDD: Can you tell me more about the professionalism of the
             Pilgrim Travelers—you know, did you have rules and
             regulations? How was the group organized along
             this . . . ?

WHITAKER: Oh, yeah. We had some rules and regulations. When
             we were calling rehearsal if you weren't there, you
             were fined. You would have to pay five dollars. And
             you can bet they were there. And we always would
             stay pretty much close together. We would talk to-
             gether and try to treat each other like brothers, you
             know. And that's the only way a group can get along
             —you got to be like brothers, and you got to be busi-
             nesslike. So, that was the Pilgrim Travelers for a long
             time. We were that way.

REDD: Do you think that all of America knows just how
             important the Pilgrim Travelers are to black musical
             history?

WHITAKER: Sometimes I wonder myself, if they really do. I'm sure
             the old-timers do—most of the old-timers do. And
             some of the younger people that are coming along
             have heard the albums, and heard our songs and most
             of them like it, you know. I just wish there would be
             more groups—I wouldn't say take the pattern after
             the Pilgrim Travelers—sing your own way, but do it
             in a more gospel and a religious way, and try and get
             more harmony with your group. I think that would be
             better.

REDD: The Soul Stirrers had a particular sound; the Dixie
             Hummingbirds had a particular sound; the Pilgrim
             Travelers had a particular sound. What made that
             particular sound?

WHITAKER: You know, that's really hard to say. I don't know.

What really inspired me to sing—you're a young man, you might remember the Golden Gates?

REDD: Oh, yes. I read about them, and have a couple of their records, but just read about them mostly.

WHITAKER: Well, that's who inspired me to sing—right here. We moved back here and bought this farm. And you couldn't even see—you had to come down through the woods to cut you a road to get through here. And the Golden Gates would come on every evening 'round about four o'clock. And I wouldn't care where I'd be, at four, I'd be heading to the house to get to the old radio—battery radio, you know? You'd turn it up as high as it'd go, and it'd keep going down. I'd almost cry as it'd go down. You couldn't hear the Golden Gates. And now that was a group. But just like I said, they didn't really mean what they were doing, you know—they were just singing. And they could sing.

REDD: You mentioned you would turn them on. About what year was this? What radio was this?

WHITAKER: Oh, that was back in 1936, '37, '38, on up through there.

REDD: Where were they coming from?

WHITAKER: They were coming out of, seems like to me, I think it was out of New York, someplace there. I just remember what station it was, CBS or NBC—I don't know which one. But anyway, it was a nationwide station. You could hear them over the whole United States. And boy, they were beautiful. They could sing.

REDD: In my research, I've come across people like the Charioteers. You mentioned the Golden Gate Quartet. What are some of the groups that you can recall that were significant and maybe just give a little bit of identification as to who they were and the part of our musical heritage of this area.

WHITAKER: Oh, sure. Just like you mentioned, the Charioteers. I remember them. They used to broadcast quite a lot, and I'd hear them. I think they would come on Sundays. And they were great in that type of singing. They were more what you call classical singers, the Charioteers were. And there was another group that wasn't quite that, but they were really—The Wings over Jordan. They were great. They did a lot for black folks' singing. They did a great deal. And there was another group—I'm trying to remember them. They used to come on every Sunday morning.

REDD: Would you be thinking about the Trumpeteers?

WHITAKER: No, not the Trumpeteers. The Trumpeteers, they come along after we were, after the Pilgrim Travelers were out there. We knew them very well. But I'm trying to think—this was an old group. It was some kind of Airs. Oh, I can't think of the name of them now, but they were great. They would come on every Sunday morning, and I'd listen to them. And I got a few pointers from them, too. They were real great. Southernairs.

REDD: Is this another group now of the Southernairs—Willie Banks and the Southernairs? Is this another group now?

WHITAKER: This is a different group altogether. A different group altogether. Do you know Banks?

REDD: I've gotten some recordings in from Song Bird out of Houston, Texas, and so that's why I'm familiar with the Southernairs.

WHITAKER: Oh, I know them very well. They're out of Jackson, Mississippi.

REDD: There were contests that gospel groups used to get into, is that right?

WHITAKER: Oh, plenty of times. Oh, yeah. Most of the time. We were never in, what you call, a contest for winning anything. We were booked up around New York quite a few times, and there'd be six or seven groups, and they'd always try to put the Pilgrim Travelers in the wringer. They wouldn't let us open up—they wouldn't call us to open up—they'd put us last. And by the help of the good Lord, we was always able to come out on top.

REDD: How would they do that? Would they try to just out-sing you? Just how did that go?

WHITAKER: Yes, that's what happened. They'd get together on that, you know. We wouldn't know about it, but we could see what was happening. They'd say, "Well, the Pilgrim Travelers been doing this and they been doing that and they've been tearing down the houses on us all the time. So let's fix them today." So, they'd get to the booking manager or whoever was doing the program, and they'd say, "Let the Pilgrim Travelers open up." Well, that was wrong because we'd open up, and they were just as bad. Then they'd say, "Well, let's put them last." Let everybody sing and do what they can do and put us up last. But so help me, the people would be waiting for us. It'd seem like they were just sitting there waiting.

REDD: So, it wasn't an animosity kind of thing—it was a challenge kind of thing.

WHITAKER: That's right, it was. And we had a lot of fun at it. We'd laugh about it afterward, and tease the groups about it. So it was all beautiful. We never had any problem with it.

REDD: Are there reunions or anything that the Pilgrim Travelers have—the original members of the Pilgrim Travelers have?

WHITAKER: Yes, we did have a reunion—a quartet singing reunion. But I think it's just about broke up now—it's just about washed out. It was great there for a while. Every year, we'd go to different cities, you know. All the groups would meet up, and we'd have a great time. But I think it's just about broken up now. After I really got out of traveling, I never heard too much about it. Of course, I hear a lot of groups, like the Pilgrim Jubilees out of Chicago, they're a very good group. They come down to Memphis quite a bit, so I drive down and listen to them.

REDD: What was the road like when you were there, and how long were you on the road with the Pilgrim Travelers?

WHITAKER: I was on the road with the Pilgrim Travelers about twelve or thirteen years. And we did very good. And then, singing was great, and the people loved it, and they would pay the money to come out and listen to it. I could see it later years, the booking managers over the country through the years, I guess they got greedy,

really, and they started booking three and four and
five groups together—trying to make a haul, you
know what I mean? And just really messing up things.
And so the people said, "Well, gee whiz, why pay a
dollar fifty or two dollars to go hear one group when
we can pay that same amount and go to hear five or
six groups?" And these booking agents have really
messed up things. And that really started the down-
grade.

REDD: I think that same thing is happening to pop music
now. Everybody seems to be screaming now.

WHITAKER: That's right. And they've started booking three and
four and five groups together, you know. And that
hurts. That hurts the groups, you know? It really
hurts. I can remember, a number of times, we'd go in
Birmingham and we would draw three or four thou-
sand people, just us—just the group. We'd go in Mobile and do that same thing. And later on, they'd start
booking two groups and three groups, and we'd draw
the same amount of people, with that many groups.
And so, I don't know. It just really messed up things.

REDD: During Black History Week, have any of the schools
in this area asked you to come around to speak to
them concerning black music?

WHITAKER: No, they haven't. Not since I've been back home. I've
only been back about two years now. And no one has
ever mentioned it to me. The only thing they mentioned to me is to come by to sing a solo.

REDD: What about some of the other guys that you may have
been in touch with? Have any writers or anyone been
by to get their stories—to document the history of
gospel music or the history of the Pilgrim Travelers?

WHITAKER: Not yet, they haven't. I've had invitations to go down
to Memphis, but they've never been here. And I've
never really had the time to go down there, because
since I've been back home, I've been very busy. And
so that's about it.

REDD: What were those invitations to go to Memphis? Do
you recall?

WHITAKER: Well, there's Oris Mays. He's a very good singer—solo singer—and also preaches. He's pastor down there and he's on TV every Sunday morning. And he wanted me to come, oh say, we might get together and do some recording. And so, I just joined this group, oh I guess about five or six months ago, and I'm trying to get them into shape. So, then, I might go down.

REDD: What was recording like then in 1947, when the Pilgrim Travelers made their first record?

WHITAKER: Oh, it was great. I enjoyed recording, and Specialty got us. And that's when the Pilgrim Travelers really started hitting them when we started recording with Specialty—"I'd Roomed With the President." And that put us on the road.

REDD: What was a recording session like? What did you do to prepare for it? And what kind of things went on in the studio to get a record ready?

WHITAKER: Oh, that's work. Believe me—that is hard work. That's just like going out on a job, maybe cutting logs or something all day long. And you'd be just exhausted. It takes you just about all day and part of the night to really do a session. And you got to really rehearse it to do it. You just can't play around with that. Now if you got a good director, he's going to listen to all your mistakes. And he'll play it back to you. And if you know anything about singing, you'll know your mistakes; he won't have to tell you, so that's what would happen. When I was with the Travelers, it looked like I'd be the one to hear all the mistakes, and I'd call them back to it. So, it was rough. You would really be exhausted when you finished a session of recording.

REDD: You mentioned J.W. Alexander. Can you tell us a little bit about J. W. Alexander?

WHITAKER: Well, I knew Jimmy just before he joined the Pilgrim Travelers, really. He was around there in Los Angeles. He wasn't doing very much. He was singing in a little group there in Los Angeles. He was singing tenor. So, after the Pilgrim Travelers lost their first manager— which was Joe Johnson—they got Alexander for their manager, and also tenor. And I think he was a great guy. He was a really smart guy—he was really shrewd, man. He'd know what was happening, he'd know how to go about it—well, he's just great, that's all. To tell you how great he is, now, if you ever go to Los Angeles, you go to Beverly Hills and look him up, and you can see what's happening. He's got a beautiful home there in Beverly Hills up in the hills, with a swimming pool down there. It's beautiful. He's great. He's doing great.

REDD: He's the manager for some of show business's top persons right now, is he not?

WHITAKER: Well, right now, I know he's got Little Richard. And he did have Sam Cooke, and then he had Lou Rawls, for a while. So I know—I'm sure he's got two or three different groups, but Little Richard I know was tops with him when I left him out there. So he's writing his own music, and got a big studio there on Sunset Boulevard there in Hollywood, and he's got five or six people working for him. So, I think he's doing all right.

REDD: One recording that I had gotten from Capitol Records was Lou Rawls with the Pilgrim Travelers, and there was also a fellow by the name of Rene Hall. Can you tell me a little bit about that gentleman?

WHITAKER: Oh, yeah. Renee—he played on quite a bit of sessions with us—with the Pilgrim Travelers. And he knew all our arrangements and just about everything about the Pilgrim Travelers. And Renee had a little band of his own which was very good. And he's a very good guy —he's very nice.

REDD: Were most of the guys originally from Los Angeles, like Ray Taylor that you talked about and Keith Barber?

WHITAKER: Well, not originally. Let's see, Kylo Turner, Keith Barber, and Ray Taylor were all from Houston, Texas. That's where they were born around Houston. And J. W., he was born in Mississippi, but he was raised in Kansas and then moved to California.

REDD: Did the record company take care of all the distribution?

WHITAKER: Oh, yes. The record company would handle all of that.

All we'd do was a recording. That was it. And very seldom would we even take any records with us. We wouldn't take any with us. The only thing we'd take were pictures.

REDD: There were some film companies operating in the late forties—black film companies. Did the Pilgrim Travelers ever make any films—appear in any motion pictures at all?

WHITAKER: No, we didn't. We never got a chance to do that. Of course, we had some offers, but it never went through, for some reason.

REDD: What about the pictures? Who would have those pictures of the Pilgrim Travelers now?

WHITAKER: Oh, I've got a couple or so. Well, they're around everywhere. We sold a whole gob of them. Just about all the old-timers got them.

REDD: Do you write music? Do you read music? How do you write your songs?

WHITAKER: No, I don't read music. I just get me a tune, and sit down and get me some words and match them up. And I'm pretty good at getting a pretty good tune. And usually it's never a discord on that. I just about know where I'm going.

REDD: Where do you see gospel music going now?

WHITAKER: Well, it's beginning to come back a little bit now, but in a different way, I think. It's not like when we were doing it. As they say, you have to change with the times, so it really has changed. And so it's beginning to come back because I notice right here in Blythville we have programs there, and it looks like more and more people are beginning to come out. And I think most of the groups realize that you cannot sing gospel songs and get around and do everything that's wrong and expect people to pay their money to come out and listen to you. You just can't do it. Now if you're going to be a rock and roller, it doesn't matter, because they'll go see you anyway. It doesn't matter. But if you're a gospel singer, they expect you to live up to that, you know, and so I think that a lot of groups are beginning to realize that. And stop all that wrongdoing and go ahead and sing. And that's that.

REDD: Do you see a time when this music, our music's going to be aired nationally on TV?

WHITAKER: I believe it will. It is now; it's happening now. Right now, I can get up every Sunday morning and turn the TV on and there are two programs coming out of Memphis—Oris Mays and his choir and there's the Jubilee Hummingbirds. They have a broadcast—a TV show, every Sunday morning. So I think it's going to be all right.

REDD: What would you like to say, taking this opportunity to say it, to young people that probably they haven't been taught in school, undoubtedly, and have missed a great deal? I feel like I've missed a great deal. Where do we start to catch up on the Soul Stirrers, the Pilgrim Travelers, the Dixie Hummingbirds, the Bells of Joy?

WHITAKER: Well, what I would say to the young people and the young groups that are singing now: the only thing to do is you can't sing like another person and be successful, really. Sing your own way. But listen. Maybe get you some records or something. The old groups got records out. Listen to them and take off of that. You don't have to sing like they sing. But sing it your way. And just be yourself. I think you'll go a long ways that way. And if you're going to sing gospel, sing gospel. If you're going to go in the pop field, go in the pop field. But don't criss-cross. Do one or the other. And I think you'll come out better.

REDD: Do you recall any articles being written on the Pilgrim Travelers in any magazines or newspaper articles?

WHITAKER: No, I don't remember. I don't recall any. There might have been, but I can't recall right now.

REDD: So all the time that the Pilgrim Travelers were really tops among black people for sure that there just wasn't that coverage being given to the gospel groups as such?

WHITAKER: That's true. It was not.

REDD: How did the Pilgrim Travelers get its name "The Pilgrim Travelers"? I know you told me you joined the group after it was started, but do you recall?

WHITAKER: No, I don't really recall. They got that name out of

Houston, Texas. They started with that name. I don't
know what was the idea of the name or what. But they
had been, you know, doing a little local singing around
Houston mostly and different places, and so they all
moved to California, and Pilgrim Travelers stuck with
them. And so, I don't know just what the idea was,
you know.

REDD: I recall that in order to break the monotony, because,
you know, singing all the time does kind of get to you,
I suppose, the Dixie Hummingbirds to liven things up
would do an imitation of all the rest of the gospel
groups called "Come On and Support Your Local
Program." The Pilgrim Travelers—what'd they do to
liven themselves up to break the monotony?

WHITAKER: Oh, we would always have a little number to sing or
something like that. Mostly with me, they would always put me out there to do it. They'd say I was the
clown of the group. Oh, a song like "Jesus Met the
Woman at the Well" and "Blessed Be the Name."
They'd always put me out to do those sort of numbers,
"I Can Do Better Than That"—songs like that.
Maybe some other group has gotten up and shouted
the place, you know, and they would call me up to do
that number. And that would get their minds back on
us, you know.

REDD: To me it's a real tragedy that no film is available
anywhere of the Pilgrim Travelers when the Pilgrim
Travelers were *the* Pilgrim Travelers in the prime,
performing. To me, that is a travesty upon the history
of the country not to have that documented.

WHITAKER: Well, it just wasn't happening in those days. The film
industry just wasn't interested in gospel, really, to tell
you the truth. They figured it was some bogus stuff.
They didn't want all that; they would call it "hollering," "squalling," all that stuff, but now it's different.
It's much different. So I think things are going to be,
in later years, I think it's going to be beautiful.

REDD: What can schools do to insure that kids know about
all these people?

WHITAKER: Well, what they should do is to get around and get—

well, I would say just like you're doing now. Get around and get some of the old singers, and let them come in and talk to the youngsters and let them know what's happening and maybe have some records or something and let them hear and let them know what's going on. You take back in those days when we were singing, you could hear a lot of white groups were singing their way, but you listen to them now—they're squalling and screaming and hollering just like we did back then. And got the movement. So you can see gospel singing—we did a lot for gospel singing.

REDD: How does that make you feel when you make that observation and know that it's true?

WHITAKER: Well, I feel pretty good inside. Really feel good inside. I just wish I could tell them how it came about.

REDD: Do you think that they really don't know? Many of them don't know?

WHITAKER: Oh, they know, because they listen to the records. If they didn't know, they couldn't do it. And you got some white groups now really singing. They're featuring bass singers just like we did. They're doing everything we did.

REDD: Only we did it first.

WHITAKER: That's right. We broke the ice.